Art and Architecture

Inside Ancient China

ANITA CROY

Sharpe Focus
an imprint of M.E. Sharpe, Inc.

First edition for the United States, its territories and dependencies,
Canada, Mexico, and Australia, published in 2009

Sharpe Focus
An imprint of M.E. Sharpe, Inc.
80 Business Park Drive
Armonk, NY 10504

www.sharpe-focus.com

Library of Congress Cataloging-in-Publication Data

Croy, Anita.
  Art and architecture / Anita Croy.
     p. cm. -- (Inside ancient China)
  Includes bibliographical references and index.
  ISBN 978-0-7656-8167-6 (hardcover : alk. paper)
  1. Art, Chinese--Juvenile literature. 2. Architecture--China--Juvenile
literature. I. Title.
  N7343.C75 2009
  709.51--dc22

                          2008030863

Editorial and design by Amber Books Ltd
Project Editor: James Bennett
Consultant Editor: Susan Whitfield
Copy Editor: Constance Novis
Picture Research: Terry Forshaw, Natascha Spargo
Design: Joe Conneally

Cover Design: Jesse M. Sanchez, M.E. Sharpe, Inc.

Printed in Malaysia

9 8 7 6 5 4 3 2 1

ABOUT THE AUTHOR
After studying modern languages, Anita Croy earned her Master's and Ph.D. degrees at
University College, University of London. Since then, she has written many books for children,
specializing in writing about Latin America and South and East Asia. Her books include
National Geographic Investigates Ancient Pueblo and *Solving the Mysteries of Macchu Picchu*.

Contents

Introduction

China is the world's oldest continuous civilization, originating in the plains and valleys of the Yellow and Yangtze rivers more than six thousand years ago. In the third century B.C.E., the separate kingdoms of China were united to form an empire. Over the centuries China was ruled by a series of ruling houses, or families, known as dynasties. The empire was governed by an emperor, who was advised by highly educated scholars and who commanded a strong army. No dynasty lasted for more than a few hundred years and several were founded by invaders, such as the Mongol Yuan Dynasty and the Manchu Qing Dynasty. Successive dynasties expanded Chinese territory, until the empire extended into the northern steppes, the western deserts, and the southern tropics, reaching the extent of the China we know today.

China was not always united. Often the fall of dynasties resulted in long periods where different groups competed for power. Dynasties sometimes overlapped, each controlling a part of China. Throughout all these periods, the rulers retained classical Chinese as the official language, and many dynasties saw great cultural and technological developments. Through ancient trade routes and political missions, Chinese culture reached the rest of Asia, Europe, and Africa. Chinese technologies—including the compass, paper, gunpowder, and printing— had a profound effect on civilization throughout Eurasia. China was, in turn, greatly influenced by its neighbors, resulting in a diverse and complex civilization.

Art and Architecture

Ancient Chinese culture was characterized by its ceramics, silk textiles, jade carvings, and unique writing system. The invention of porcelain at the end of the first millennium C.E. was a remarkable breakthrough in technology that European craftsmen strived to replicate for many centuries. Europeans also sought to discover the secret of silk and to weave the complex brocades that were traded along the Silk Road. Jade, a beautiful and very hard mineral, was already being finely carved in China in around 2000 B.C.E. The carver's skills were extended to many other materials, including ivory, rhinoceros horn, bamboo, wood, and stone.

Chinese skills with the brush first developed into a unique method of artistic handwriting called calligraphy. Some of the earliest Chinese paintings, preserved in tombs, show Buddhist themes, and many arts in ancient China were influenced by skills and materials from its neighbors. Chinese architecture, however, is generally unique in style, and although most ancient buildings were made of wood and have long since disappeared, tomb structures and paintings tell us much about early Chinese architecture.

The Main Dynasties of China

Shang   c. 1600–c. 1050 B.C.E.
Zhou   c. 1050–221 B.C.E.

The Zhou Dynasty can be divided into:
>   Western Zhou   1050–771 B.C.E.
>   Eastern Zhou   770–221 B.C.E.

>   *The Eastern Zhou Dynasty can also be divided into the following periods:*
>>   Spring and Autumn Period   770–476 B.C.E.
>>   Warring States Period   475–221 B.C.E.

Qin   221–206 B.C.E.
Han   206 B.C.E.–220 C.E.

From 221 C.E. to 589 C.E., different regions of China were ruled by several different dynasties and emperors in a period of disunity.

Sui   589–618 C.E.
Tang   618–907 C.E.

There was another period of disunity between the Tang and Song dynasties.

Song   960–1279 C.E.
Yuan   1279–1368 C.E.
Ming   1368–1644 C.E.
Qing   1644–1911 C.E.

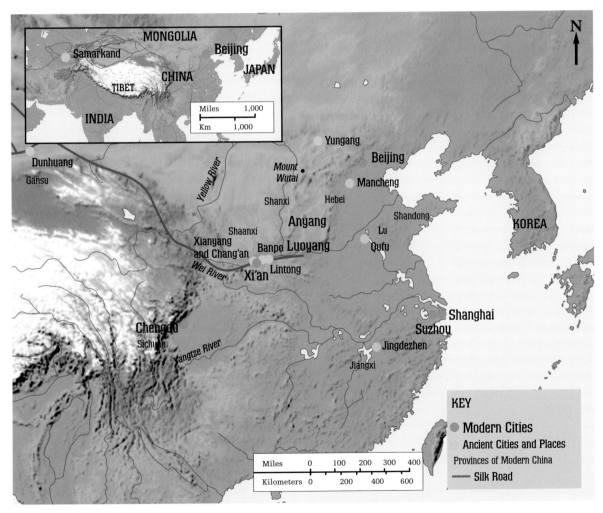

This map shows the major present-day and ancient cities and regions mentioned throughout this book, along with the Silk Road between Luoyang in the Yellow River valley and the Mediterranean Sea.

Chapter One

Painting and Calligraphy

The foundation of Chinese art was calligraphy, the writing of Chinese characters in a balanced and beautiful form. According to legend, an official in the court of the mythological ruler Huang Di (whose name translates as Yellow Emperor) supposedly invented Chinese writing 4,000 years ago. He created a series of written characters that were inspired by bird and animal tracks.

Calligraphy goes beyond writing, in that the characters are seen as art and not primarily as words. In fact, in some forms of calligraphy it is difficult to even read the individual characters. Scribes were trained to copy manuscripts in a certain style and were expected to produce beautiful and clear writing, but the calligrapher produced art.

When the First Emperor Qin (*Chin*) (259–210 B.C.E.) unified China in 221 B.C.E., one of his many radical reforms to bring the diverse territories and people under his control was to order that writing be integrated into a single system. By the 220s B.C.E., writing was highly developed. The characters were standardized but complex. It took a high level of skill and constant practice to produce an elegant text. Emperor Huizong (*Hweh-tzong*) (1082–1135 C.E.) was at the forefront of the transformation of calligraphy from writing into an art form. He developed a new form of calligraphy known as "slender gold." Calligraphers used a soft, flexible brush to write their characters. The brush hair

The landscape painting "Mount Kuanglu" dates from the Five Dynasties era (907–960 C.E.) and was painted by Jing Hao on silk with water and ink. He was following the Tang Dynasty (618–907 C.E.) tradition of emphasizing landscape in his work.

Qin Seal Script

During the time of the Qin Dynasty (221–206 B.C.E.), a new way of writing known as Small Seal Script was devised. It contained nearly 12,000 characters, or words. It was developed from the many regional scripts that existed, and served as the model for later scripts. It differed from the earlier Big Seal Script because fewer brushstrokes were needed to compose each character. Seal script was notable for its regular size, with each brushstroke having the same thickness. This made it easier to standardize the Chinese characters and for it to be read by officials throughout the empire.

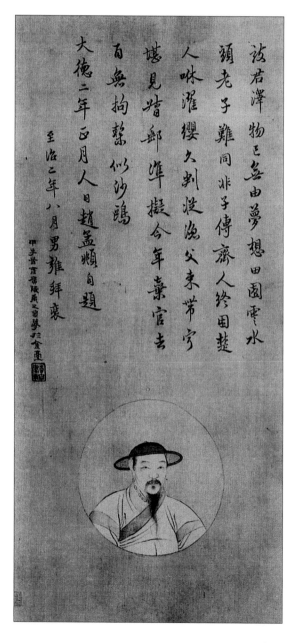

came from animals and was tied with silk and fitted into a bamboo or wooden tube. Pine soot mixed with lampblack from burned plants made the ink that the calligraphers used. Animal glue was added to the mixture and then it was molded into a stick or cake. Sometimes the mixture was made into different shapes, such as a dragon. It was very good ink that did not run once it was dry.

Calligraphers ground the ink sticks or cakes with a little water on an ink stone, which was made from stone or pottery. The smoother the stone, the easier it was to grind the ink into a smooth liquid.

The beautifully decorated inkstones and brushes made for use by ancient Chinese calligraphers show the importance attached to the art of calligraphy. During the tenth century, the four articles used by calligraphers—brushes, paper, ink, and ink stone—became known as "the four treasures of the scholar's studio."

The calligrapher Zhao Mengfu (1254–1322 C.E.) helped to create a new style of calligraphy during the Yuan Dynasty (1279–1368 C.E.). This is a particularly good example of his work.

Painting

The earliest examples of painting in China date back 6,000 years to when cave dwellers painted shapes and figures on the walls of caves using charcoal pigments. Later, the pictures had evolved into more decorative images of spirals, zigzags, and dots, in addition to animals.

There were two main kinds of ancient Chinese painting. One kind involves painting on portable media, such as paper and silk. The other kind of painting is on fixed structures, such as on the wall and bricks of ancient tombs, religious structures, and palaces. Our knowledge of the development of painting comes from ongoing archaeological excavations, which have revealed paintings on the walls of ancient tombs and the occasional wooden temple that has survived. Large numbers of paintings on paper and silk have survived along with highly decorated lacquered objects.

Portable paintings were done on scrolls that were either horizontal or vertical. Vertical scrolls were hung on walls while horizontal scrolls could be unrolled little by little and viewed on a table. Smaller pictures, painted on little squares of paper, were used to decorate objects such as hand-held fans or collected in picture albums.

Artists could not afford to paint for a living without a patron to buy their finished works. Only religious and imperial institutions could afford to pay artists to create works on a large scale. Emperors employed the best artists of their generation to produce magnificent pieces of work that fulfilled not just their desire to be surrounded by beauty but also a propaganda function, showing the emperor's role in the world.

Important and rich people had their portrait painted during their lifetime. After their death, these paintings were used as the basis for ancestor portraits. The images were very formal

Wang Hui (1632–1717 c.e.) painted this silk handscroll using ink and paint. Horizontal scroll paintings like Wang Hui's "Fishing in Willow Brook" shows a landscape combined with a poem on the same scroll.

Seals

The imperial Chinese court used a wide range of seals for different purposes. For example, collector's seals were used to identify the ownership of a work of art, and were always printed in red ink. The name of the owner or a favorite quotation could be used as the seal. It was also possible for a painting to have more than one seal. This would show its different owners as well as different admirers. The seal became an important part of the work of art and could substantially increase its value. The seals were made from stone or wood with the Chinese characters etched on them in a reverse image and then printed in red ink.

and would usually show a man dressed in his official robes seated on a chair. These large portrait scrolls would be brought out at New Year and hung in the main room of the house, where the family would making offerings to their ancestors.

Landscape Painting

The great age of landscape painting took place starting in the third century and lasted until the twelfth century C.E. During this period, landscape painting was more highly regarded than any other form of painting. Chinese artists concentrated on creating a perfect image of nature long before any artists in the West. The importance of nature in painting may have been

inspired by the different philosophical beliefs of Daoism and Confucianism. Daoism, in particular, stressed the small place human beings occupied in the natural world, and many paintings show soaring mountain peaks with very small human figures going about their everyday business, dominated by the mountains.

Several styles of painting developed among the artists of the Song Dynasty (960–1279 C.E.). Many artists had fled to the mountains during the disorder at the end of the Tang Dynasty. They painted images of great mountains dwarfing human figures, reflecting their experiences.

An Imperial Painting Academy was established at the start of the Song Dynasty which produced paintings on a smaller scale,

Three Schools of Thought

Chinese culture was influenced by three main schools of thought: Confucianism, Daoism, and Buddhism. Often people would lean toward one school at different times in their lives. Confucianism believed man's nature was naturally good, and stressed harmony in families and by extension across society. Daoism regarded harmony with nature as the ultimate good and sought freedom from convention. Buddhism was a religion from India and taught that people would be reincarnated (born again) in future lives and that by doing good deeds they could hope for a better next life.

This horizontal scroll, titled "Royal Territory," is just over 39 feet (12 meters) in length. Painted on silk, it is the work of the Song Dynasty artist Wang Ximeng (1096–1119 C.E.).

painted with great skill. When the empire split into Northern and Southern dynasties, the Academy continued in the south and its painters produced very descriptive paintings, often of flowers and objects, which where used on fans and scrolls.

Guo Xi (c. 1001–c. 1090)

One of the most important paintings of ancient China was "Early Spring" by Guo Xi. He worked in northern China during the Song Dynasty (960–1279 C.E.) and produced "Early Spring" in 1072. This painting perhaps best captures the most important ideas of Chinese landscape painting. It is all the more significant because Guo Xi wrote down his ideas about what made the ideal painting and these influenced subsequent generations of painters.

"Early Spring" is one of the earliest surviving examples of a black ink painting without other colors, and Guo Xi used a technique that dates from the eighth century. The painting shows mountains, one of the most important symbols of Chinese art, along with pools of water and waterfalls with trees growing on the mountainsides. Unlike his predecessors, Guo Xi only painted landscapes—the few figures of people in his paintings are tiny and insignificant. It was his concentration on landscapes that helped make this the most popular subject in paintings of the eleventh century.

Guo Xi wrote his theories on art in his book *Lofty Ambition in Forests and Streams.* He claimed that great art was the work of a great artist and not just inspired by the external landscape. Instead, work came from the artist's heart or mind. He added to existing theories on art with his discussion of "three types of distance": high, deep, and level. Guo Xi's writings suggest that he was able to paint whatever and whenever he wanted. However, this was not true. As a court painter, his duty was to the emperor.

Gardens

The creation of a Chinese garden was considered a work of art comparable to a painting. While the design and planning of buildings followed strict principles, the design of gardens was one area that allowed freedom of expression. A traditional Chinese garden or *yuan* (this word translates as "garden" or "park") was intended to resemble a three-dimensional landscape painting that included hills and lakes with islands floating on them. Trees were encouraged to grow into interesting gnarled shapes, and plants and flowers grew in natural clumps, as in the wild. The gardens were planned to take into account changing vistas depending on where the onlooker stood. Bridges and pavilions featured extensively in Chinese gardens as sites for contemplation. During the Ming Dynasty (1368–1644 C.E.), gardens were popular places for literary meetings where the educated people met to read and write poetry. The First Emperor Qin, who ruled from 221 to 210 B.C.E., built one of the earliest gardens for which records exist. This huge garden, which was outside his capital Xianyang (*Shee'an-yang*) near present-day Xi'an (*Shee'an*), was said to have a circumference of 93 miles (150 kilometers). It included an imperial game reserve as well as a huge artificial lake, which was used by the imperial navy and as a reservoir. The park, Shanglinyuan, of which little remains, set a standard for other imperial parks to follow.

Gardens became popular during the Han Dynasty (206 B.C.E.–220 C.E.), and both private and imperial gardens were built. Imperial family members created their own private gardens while officials also produced some of the most magnificent gardens. One official, Shi Zhengzhi (*Shuh-jung-tzuh*), created the Wangshiyuan (Garden of the Master of the Fishing Nets) in Suzhou (*Soo-Joe*), Jiangsu province, during the Song Dynasty (960–1279 C.E.).

"Early Spring" is one of the most famous of all Chinese landscape paintings. Guo Xi (1001–1090 C.E.) painted it in 1072, and it is one of the earliest surviving works painted in ink. It was painted on silk, which has yellowed over time. A remote landscape is depicted, the Daoist idea of paradise.

The Gardens of Suzhou

Suzhou, close to Shanghai, is often called the Venice of the East because of its network of canals. It was once filled with famous gardens, built between the tenth and late nineteenth centuries. Many of them were private gardens built by retired generals, officials, scholars, and painters. Each garden, no matter how small the space was, contained the essential elements of a Chinese garden: water, rocks (sometimes piled high to resemble mountains), and plants. Poetry and calligraphy were also considered vital elements, so the many pavilions, bridges, and meeting places in the garden had poetic names. The structures were usually linked to a literary quotation with calligraphy carved over the doorway of the entrances.

The Lingering Garden is one of the four most famous gardens in Suzhou. Originally built during the Ming Dynasty (1368–1644 C.E.) as a private garden, it is now a UNESCO World Heritage site.

900 C.E.		1100 C.E.		1300 C.E.	
Period of Disunity		Song Dynasty 960–1279 C.E.		Yuan Dynasty 1279–1368 C.E.	
"Mount Kuanglu"	"Early Spring," 1072	Wang Ximeng 1096–1119 C.E.		Zhao Mengfu 1254–1322 C.E.	
	Canglang Pavilion		Garden of the Master of the Fishing Nets		Shizilin Garden

The Canglangting is the oldest garden in Suzhou, dating from the Song Dynasty (906–1127 C.E.). The scholar Sun Shunqin designed the garden during his retirement.

Though the tiny Wangshiyuan (Garden of the Master of the Fishing Nets) dates from the Song Dynasty (960–1279 C.E.), many alterations were made over the following centuries. This garden was inspired by the words of a fisherman and contained, among other structures, the "Pavilion for Viewing Pines and Enjoying Paintings," the "Late Spring Abode," the "Hold to Peace Mansion," and the "Lute Chamber." The Canglangting (Pavilion of Dark Blue Waves) dates from the Song Dynasty (960–1127 C.E.) and was famed for its natural scenery. The Yipu (Garden of Skill) was built during the Ming Dynasty (1368–1644 C.E.) and was once filled with medicinal plants. The Shizilin (Forest of Stone Lions) was originally built in 1342 C.E. as part of a temple complex. A major feature of the garden is the many oddly shaped lake rocks covered in moss that remind the visitor of mountains and forests.

The greatest garden in Suzhou, and perhaps China, is Zhouzhengyuan (Garden of the Humble Administrator). This large garden was originally laid out in the sixteenth century and covers an impressive 13 acres (52,000 square meters). The lake takes up around one-fifth of the garden and has many streams and bridges. Pavilions are dotted around the garden to give the visitor as many different views as possible.

1500 C.E.	1700 C.E.
Ming Dynasty 1368–1644 C.E.	Qing Dynasty 1644–1911 C.E.

PAINTING AND CALLIGRAPHY

Garden of the Humble Administrator Lingering Garden	
Garden of Skill	*GARDENS*

Chapter Two

Chinese Crafts

Ancient Chinese culture placed a strong emphasis on its crafts. As soon as people settled in communities, they started to make objects that were not strictly for functional use. Unfortunately, because many of the early objects were made from fragile materials they have long since disappeared. Bronze was the first sturdy material to be used in large quantities and the many thousands of bronze artifacts that have been discovered chart the development of bronze working. In the same way, jade and ceramics have survived in large numbers.

Pottery and Porcelain

China's ancient culture can be traced back to the settlements that developed close to the two main rivers that cross China, the Yangtze River in the south and the Yellow River in the north. Around 9,000 years ago, farmers settled by both rivers, growing cereal crops in the north and rice in the south. As communities became more settled around 8,000 years ago, they started to work with the clay and make pots both for daily use and for ceremonial occasions. Ceramics continued to develop for thousands of years.

Remains of clay pots and bronze tools date early pot making to at least 4000 B.C.E. Outside the Neolithic village of Banpo on the outskirts of Xi'an, in Shaanxi (*Shaarn-shee*) province, archaeologists have found six kilns (ovens that heat to a high temperature) for firing pots, which the villagers had shaped by hand. People buried their dead with ceramic bowls while small children were buried in ceramic jars with lids on.

This pottery jar is typical of the ceramic ware produced during the Han Dynasty (206 B.C.E.– 220 C.E.). The glaze is unfired but the colors are still vivid after more than 2,000 years.

Over the centuries, ceramic production improved and changed as technology introduced new techniques and styles. It gradually became possible to fire pots at higher temperatures. During the Han Dynasty (206 B.C.E.–220 C.E.) there were several advances, including the use of the potter's wheel and crushed-lead and ash-baked glaze. The technology continued to improve. By the Tang Dynasty (618–907 C.E.) ceramics became more extravagant and highly prized.

Ceramics of Banpo

In 1953, workmen digging the foundations for a factory accidentally discovered the site of the village of Banpo. The village was probably occupied around 5000–4000 B.C.E., and was located in the fertile valleys of the Wei and Middle Yellow rivers. The ceramics uncovered at this ancient site are impressive examples of Yangshao (painted) pottery. The pots were crafted by hand but may have been finished using an early type of potter's wheel. Made from red clay, the pots used for burial were finished with black, white, and red designs. Pots used every day, such as bowls, dishes, and *amphorae* (jugs or vases with two handles), were usually left unpainted but sometimes decorated with cord, mat, or basketwork patterns.

The painted pots found in the tombs display a progression in design from shapes of fish, human faces and small deer, to geometric designs taken from the shape of the fish.

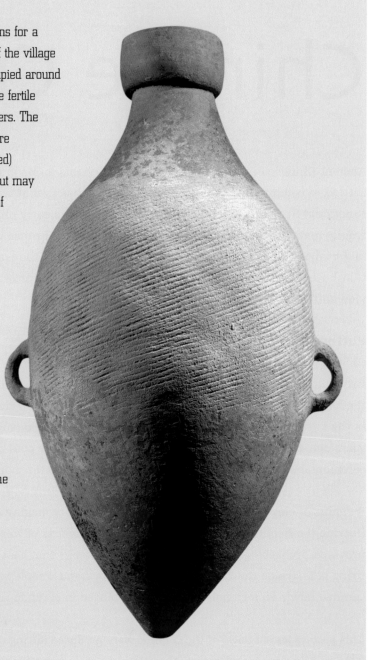

This amphora dates back to 4800 B.C.E. Although it was unpainted, there is evidence of decoration on the clay surface.

A new type of pottery appeared, known as *sancai* (three-colored). Bright yellow, green, and white glazes were used to decorate the clay. Tang potters made not only traditionally shaped pots, such as bowls and vases, but also more unusually shaped objects. Ceramic camels, inspired by the real-life camels that carried goods along the Silk Road between China and Europe, were popular. Many of the finest glazed figures were put in tombs. Horses, camels, *lokapala* (Buddhist guardians), and other exotic figures accompanied the deceased for use in the afterlife. Such large numbers of these figures have been excavated that archaeologists think there were large-scale industries devoted to making and glazing the figures.

A very popular ceramic ware of the later Tang Dynasty rulers was a green and white pottery featuring a new kind of glaze called *celadon*. The transparent crackle glaze, produced in a large number of colors, was painted onto porcelain and white clay. The finish was so popular that ceramics decorated with the celadon glaze came to be known as celadons. It was originally used solely for the imperial court during the Song Dynasty (960–1279 C.E.), but later became popular not just in China but also across the East, particularly in Japan and Korea.

The popularity of ceramics during the Tang Dynasty led to large numbers of kilns to fire the pottery being built, particularly in northern China and south of the Yangtze River. Specialty kilns were built that could fire a wide variety of glazes and ceramic

Celadon Glazes

Adding iron oxide to a glaze mixture made celadon glazes, which could be created in a wide variety of colors. The finished color depended on the thickness of the glaze and the type of clay used. The most famous and popular celadon glazes were a shade of green meant to copy jade. The cracked appearance was caused by a glaze defect during the high-temperature firing, but this is what made it extremely valuable.

This vase was produced during the Yuan Dynasty (1279–1368 C.E.). It is a fine example of *celadon* glazing.

A pottery vessel made in the shape of an animal head. Possibly used as a water vessel, it was highly decorated with abstract patterns. The vessel was excavated in 1961 in Shanxi province and dates from the Spring and Autumn Period (770–475 B.C.E.).

figures and by the end of the dynasty they were producing ceramics fired at very high temperatures. This, in turn, led to more sophisticated pottery being produced during the Song Dynasty.

During the Song Dynasty (960–1279 C.E.), a distinct northern and southern pottery emerged and kilns became industrial in scale. More often than not, it was the potters in the north who produced new glazes and techniques, which were then copied in southern China. A new middle-class emerged who could afford to buy the ceramics and fueled the demand for them. At the same time, merchants exported ceramics as far away as the Middle East as worldwide interest in Chinese ceramics grew. The type of pottery produced varied from bowls fired at high temperatures to glazed objects in an olive-green shade. Thick bowls were also produced, which were glazed in iron-black and iron-brown finishes, and these were used by Japanese monks.

The Invention of Porcelain

By the end of the Song Dynasty (960–1279 C.E.), potters were using a mixture of minerals fired at very high temperatures to create almost translucent white wares. The potters of the Yuan Dynasty (1279–1368 C.E.) started to use a special kind of clay called kaolin in the mixture. The ceramic produced became known in the West as porcelain. Porcelain was finer, smoother, whiter, and more translucent than other ceramics. To produce it, a specific mixture of minerals including kaolin requires a firing temperature as high as 2336–2552°F (1280–1400°C). Porcelain soon became very highly prized worldwide and potters in Europe tried to discover how it was made but did not have the skills or kilns to produce it for many centuries. In the meantime, the Chinese exported boatloads of ceramics, usually much coarser than the ones they produced for their own use.

By this time one of the most productive kilns in China was in a town called Jingdezhen (*Jing-duh-jun*) in Jiangxi. It had started production of white Tang wares but by the Ming Dynasty (1368–1644 C.E.) the kilns were producing vast quantities of porcelain to meet the demands for the highly sought-after bowls, cups, vases, and plates that were shipped across the world. The

Made from fine porcelain, this vase dates from the Yuan Dynasty (1279–1368 C.E.). Its blue and white finish became very popular during the following Ming Dynasty. The vase is decorated with flowers and trees, which were popular images for porcelain.

Division of Labor

To meet worldwide demand, a large workforce was required, and soon porcelain was being mass-produced. This meant that no single artist created a piece of porcelain from molding the raw material to firing the glaze. Instead, separate workshops were involved in different parts of the process with as many as seventy people working on a single object in many different workshops. In addition to the thousands of skilled workers, porcelain production involved many thousands of low-skilled workers during the peak summer season.

clay for the pots was found in large quantities close to Jingdezhen, which was conveniently located close to forests, which supplied the wood needed to fire the kilns, and rivers, along which the finished porcelain could be transported in boats.

Under the emperor's patronage, porcelain production in Jingdezhen grew rapidly. In the peak year for production, 1577 C.E., the palace commissioned 96,500 small pieces and 56,600 large pieces, as well as more than 20,000 other pieces to be used in sacrificial ceremonies. The palace kept many of the pieces for its own use but many were also given as gifts to conquered states in return for their tribute. The imperial court would only accept the highest quality wares, and archaeologists have discovered thousands of pieces of porcelain deliberately destroyed because they did not meet the required standards.

The artisans of Jingdezhen produced many different shapes and designs of porcelain but became most famous for pieces decorated in the distinctive blue glaze and polychrome (multicolored) enamels. Designs included pictures of dragons, birds, fish, and children playing. The designs on some pieces of porcelain even told stories, and these were very popular outside China. Customers in Japan, southeast Asia, western Asia, and eventually Europe all wanted the porcelain. When, during the seventeenth century, the imperial court's demand for porcelain declined, the overseas markets took over. The Japanese wanted small dishes, cups, and bowls to use in their tea ceremonies while the Europeans wanted large dinner services. The popularity of porcelain, which became known as "china" in Europe because of its place of origin, grew after 1604. The Dutch captured two Portuguese ships laden with around 200,000 pieces of porcelain, and then sold the precious cargo. King James I of England, and King Henri IV of France, as well as the Grand Duke of Tuscany, all put in bids to purchase the porcelain.

Jade Carving

Jade has always been one of the most highly sought-after stones in China. Prized since the earliest times of ancient China, it was known as the "stone of the heavens." The quality and color of jade vary greatly. Although the stone comes in colors that range from soft green, red, and gray to brown and black, the most valued was white. Jade is a form of a mineral called nephrite (*NEF-right*), the best quality of which is very scarce.

The ancient Chinese had long believed that jade had special powers and it was associated with immortality. They put jade in tombs to preserve the body and protect it from evil spirits. During the Han Dynasty (206 B.C.E.–220 C.E.) important people were buried in suits made from pieces of jade held together by threads of gold and silver. Jade was also associated with virtue and goodness, and for the ancient Chinese the phrase "as good as jade" was the same as the common saying "as good as gold."

Where Does Jade Come From?

Jade is a form of an extremely hard mineral known as nephrite (*NEF-right*). Nephrite forms deep inside the Earth's crust as a result of the combination of minerals and changes in the pressure and temperature of the Earth's layers. Because nephrite only forms under very specific conditions, the high-quality nephrite needed to make jade is very rare. Over millions of years, nephrite is pushed toward the Earth's surface until it finally emerges. Then it lies exposed, baked by the sun and battered by wind and rain. Pieces eventually break off and, once they have been collected, they can be worked on to produce what we know as jade.

The Dihedral Jade Cup is a magnificent example of the high degree of craftsmanship that jade carvers achieved during the Han Dynasty (206 C.E.–220 C.E.). The practice of burying jade with the dead became popular because people believed jade would guarantee them life after death.

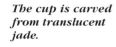

The surface of the cup is illustrated with carved designs.

The cup is carved from translucent jade.

A carved dragon wraps around the body of the cup.

The Dihedral Jade Cup is only about 6 inches (15 cm) tall.

Bi and Cong

The *bi* was a jade disk with a circular hole in the middle. Often found in tombs placed on the lower part of the deceased's body, archaeologists are unsure of its meaning although one suggestion is that it was placed there to guard against evil spirits. Some of the *bi* are more than 8 inches (20 cm) in width.

Cong were rectangular-shaped oblong containers with a circular hole in the middle, also found in burial chambers. These were placed on the chest of the deceased. Made of jade, their function also remains a mystery.

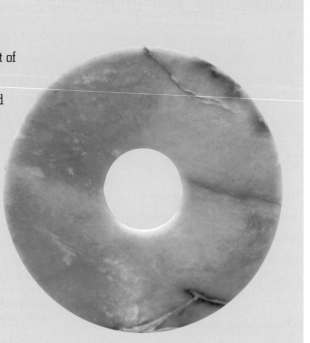

This large, pale olive green jade *bi* dates from the Zhou Dynasty (c. 1050–221 B.C.E.).

Unlike other stones, jade is extremely hard and cannot be carved. It has to be abraded, which means it must be rubbed with sand to shape and smooth it. Wooden and leather polishing wheels were used to make the jade shine. It is an extremely long process that requires a great deal of skill.

Tools made from nephrite during the Neolithic Period (10,000–2000 B.C.E.) have been found. The oldest tools date back to 4500 B.C.E. As well as being used to make ceremonial weapons and tools, Neolithic peoples fashioned jade into ornaments and small animals. People from the Liangzhu culture (dating back to about 2500 B.C.E.) used two specific pieces of jade for ritual purposes. One was a disk known as a *bi (bee)*, and the other was the *cong*. Archaeologists have discovered hundreds of *bi* and *cong* in ancient tombs. Some of them were decorated with carvings. Once bronze making developed, the use of jade became less widespread but still continued throughout ancient China.

Bronze Making

Much of what we know about the ancient Chinese comes from the thousands of bronze artifacts that have been discovered in tombs and ancient valleys. For the historian, bronze has a great advantage over other materials used by the ancient Chinese because it is virtually indestructible. Unlike in other early cultures, ancient Chinese bronze daggers and axes were

How Was Bronze Cast?

Mixing the metals copper and tin, sometimes adding in lead, makes bronze. There were two main ways of casting bronze, known as the piece-mold and lost-wax methods. In the piece-mold technique, used by the people of the Shang Dynasty (c. 1600–1050 B.C.E.), a model of the object was first made. Then, soft clay was pressed around the model, on the inside and out, so that an impression of every surface was captured. Once the clay was dry, the workers carefully cut it from the model. They were left with a reverse copy of the final shape. The clay was then fired in a kiln like any piece of pottery. The pieces were fitted into a frame and metal workers poured the molten (liquid) bronze into the mold. After the bronze cooled and hardened, the mold was broken to reveal the object.

The other method, the lost-wax technique, was used by later Chinese dynasties. First, a wax model of the object was made. The wax model was then covered with clay to make a shell of the model's shape. When the clay was fired in the hot kiln, the wax melted to leave a space for the molten bronze. It was poured in, left to cool, and then the clay broken away to reveal the bronze object.

not used as weapons but for religious purposes. Impressive bronze weapons, as well as stunning ritual vessels, were created for the first time ever during the Shang Dynasty (c. 1600–1050 B.C.E.). Bronze vessels in the shape of animals, including tigers, elephants, rhinoceroses, sheep, and oxen were also made at this time.

The ritual containers were used for making offerings of food and wine during prayers and ceremonies. Pots were made to cook food while jugs were used to hold wine, and goblets were made for drinking the wine. Many of the bronze designs, found in tombs of the Shang Dynasty, were made for the rituals, and they copied earlier designs. For example, tripods were copies of older three-legged pots. Four-legged pots were for use by the royal family. Many of the Shang bronze vessels were decorated with a *taotie* (face), the meaning of which remains a mystery. Some historians think the *taotie* was meant to frighten away evil spirits, while others thought that it was a dragon for good luck or even an abstract design that did not mean anything.

This bronze vessel in the shape of an elephant was used to hold wine. It was produced between 1300 and 1030 B.C.E. during the Shang Dynasty.

The crane, with its long legs and neck, is a symbol of longevity in China.

This square-shaped bronze vase is one of a pair. Made during the Spring and Autumn Period (770–476 B.C.E.), it is 40 inches (102 cm) high.

On top of the vase is an open lotus flower with a crane sitting on top.

The sides of the vessel are decorated with dragons.

5000–4000 B.C.E.	2000 B.C.E.		1000 B.C.E.	
Neolithic Period		Shang Dynasty c. 1600–1050 B.C.E.		Zhou Dynasty c. 1050–221 B.C.E.
Banpo pottery		Bronze weapons, vessels, and animals produced		
		Jade *bi*		

Cloisonné Enamel Technique

During the fourteenth and fifteenth centuries, new techniques in decorating metal objects were invented. They combined the techniques of bronze and porcelain making along with traditional Chinese painting.

What Is Cloisonné?

Cloisonné (*KLWA-zonnay*) is the name given to a way of creating designs using colored enamel to decorate an object. The name comes from a French word, *cloisons* (*KLWA-zonz*), meaning partitions. Paste is set in shapes made by copper and bronze wires and then fired in a kiln. After the paste is put in place, it is colored using metallic oxide and painted into the marked areas of the design. Then the container has to be fired at a low temperature (compared with ceramic firing) of 1472°F (800°C). The enamel tends to shrink when heated so the process has to be repeated until the design is completely filled in. The next stage is to rub the surface until the edges of the *cloisons* can be seen. To finish, the edges, the inside of the pot, and the base are then covered with a thin layer of gold.

History of Cloisonné

Cloisonné first appeared in Beijing during the Yuan Dynasty (1279–1368 C.E.). It developed during the Ming Dynasty (1368–1644 C.E.), particularly during the Jingtai Period (1426–1456 C.E.), because Emperor Zhu Qiyu (*Joo-chee-yoo*) (1428–1457 C.E.) was very interested in bronze-casting techniques and wanted his objects to be finished in different colors. The emperor ordered most of the articles for his daily use to be made of cloisonné. Cloisonné also became fashionable among ordinary people; the most popular bright blue glaze was known as "Jingtai Blue."

During the Qing Dynasty (1644–1911 C.E.), cloisonné improved and reached its peak. Colors became more sophisticated. They were more delicate and the metal wires, known as filigrees, were more flexible to produce a better finish. The kind of objects made in cloisonné increased to include snuff bottles, folding screens, incense burners, tables, chairs, chopsticks, and bowls. Cloisonné was originally intended for use in temples and palaces. Its bright colors and patterns were not considered suitable for scholars' houses, which were known for their subdued, quiet atmosphere.

1 C.E.				1000 C.E.			1500 C.E.
Han Dynasty 206 B.C.E.–220 C.E.	**Period of Disunity**		**Tang Dynasty** 618–907 C.E.	**Song Dynasty** 960–1279 C.E.		**Ming Dynasty** 1368–1644 C.E.	
Qin Dynasty 221–206 B.C.E.		**Sui Dynasty** 589–618 C.E.			**Yuan Dynasty** 1279–1368 C.E.		
Potter's wheel introduced			**Celadon invented**		**Cloisonné introduced**	**Production at Jingdezhen peaks** 1577 C.E.	
Dihedral Jade Cup		**Longmen Seated Buddha** 672–675 C.E.			**Porcelain invented**		

This style of ceramic vessel is known as a moon flask. This example of Cloisonné enamel dates from the Qing Dynasty (1644–1911 C.E.).

Sculpture

Sculpture has been a vital part of ancient Chinese culture from the very earliest settlers along the Yellow and Yangtze rivers, who made pottery and clay figures, to the sophisticated figures of the terracotta army of First Emperor Qin (259–210 B.C.E.), and the figures of the Ming Dynasty (1368–1644 C.E.) and Qing Dynasty (1644–1911 C.E.). In addition to freestanding sculpture, wall sculptures decorated tombs and palaces.

The surprise discovery of the tomb of First Emperor Qin, at Xi'an, Shaanxi province, with its amazing terracotta army, was one of the most magnificent archaeological finds of the century when it was revealed in March 1974. The underground chamber containing an army of at least 7,000 life-sized terracotta soldiers from the late third century B.C.E. has greatly increased our understanding of Chinese sculpture. The figures of ceramic cavalrymen and chariots, all arranged in battle formation, are notable because they have mass-produced body parts yet each figure is unique.

These magnificent terracotta warriors and horses stand in the same position in which they were placed at the death of Emperor Qin in the late third century B.C.E. No two warriors are the same.

Buddhism brought another important form of sculpture to China. The prosperous Tang Dynasty (618–907 C.E.) developed Buddhist art to its highest level. Skilled sculptors used stone to carve huge figures of the Buddha, and iron replaced bronze in the casting of figures. Terracotta figures were also glazed. During the Song Dynasty (960–1279 C.E.), as Buddhism declined, monumental Chinese sculpture ceased to be a major art form and fewer and fewer figures were carved.

Stone Sculptures

Unlike Western sculpture, Chinese sculpture did not make a distinction between religious and nonreligious sculpture. Chinese sculpture was very closely linked to religion. Beginning in the Neolithic Period (10,000–2000 B.C.E.) and onward, sculptures made from jade, marble, rock crystal, and stone were found at sites of sacrificial ceremonies, and eventually stone animals, such as lions, guarded tombs alongside imaginary animals like the *qilin* (unicorn). The spirit paths of the Tang Dynasty (618–907 C.E.) were lined with stone *stelae* (slabs with inscriptions carved on them), and statues and the tombs of the nobility were decorated with stone friezes (bands of sculpted decoration).

However, it was the arrival of Buddhism in China from the first century that heralded a golden age of stone sculpture. Sculpture was often considered a lesser art form, but some of the most beautiful of all Chinese sculpture was produced for Buddhist temples. Thousands of workers, including stonemasons, potters, metalworkers, and painters, were employed to decorate the many Buddhist temples and monasteries that flourished. The massive seated Buddha in the cave temple complexes at Dunhuang (*Doo'un-hwang*) in Gansu province, which was sculpted between 712 and 781 C.E. and is 100 feet (33 meters) in height, and the seated and standing Buddhas in Yungang, Shaanxi province (46 feet [14 meters] and 49 feet [15 meters] in height respectively), show the high level of craftsmanship reached in the fourth and fifth centuries.

One of the most outstanding Buddhist cave temples is the Longmen Caves in Henan province, near the Yi River. The caves were carved over centuries and number more than 1,300, and also include many smaller niches. Almost 100,000 statues were carved for the caves. These include the Seated Buddha of the Feng Xian Si (Ancestor-Worshipping Cave), which was carved between 672 and 675 C.E. and is 56 feet (17 meters) high. By the end of the sixth century, there was a change in the style. They became more rounded and the draping of their robes was shown. The peak period for Buddhist art came during the Tang Dynasty. The faces of the statues acquired a serene expression and the robes became more elegant and refined.

The Seated Buddha of the Feng Xian Si (Ancestor-Worshipping Cave) was carved for the Empress Wu Zetian. It is the largest and most splendid in the Longmen Caves and is considered the high point of Tang carving.

Chapter Three

Music

Music has occupied a central role in Chinese life for thousands of years. In ancient Chinese writing, the word for *yue* (music) was written with a Chinese character that also meant, "joy," "pleasure," and "entertainment."

Music was understood by the ancient Chinese to be not just the sounds made by musical instruments but also the sounds of the universe. The ancient Chinese believed the earth breathed and the sounds of its breathing inspired all other music. Since an integral part of living a good life was respect for the symbolic order of a harmonious cosmos, music was sometimes considered more important than rituals and ceremonies. The poet Ruan Ji, who belonged to a group of Daoist intellectuals who met in a forest near Luoyang to play music and compose songs, said, *"Music is the substance of the universe, the nature of beings; it is in the union of this substance, and the agreement with this nature, that harmony is achieved."*

The ancient Chinese believed that sound was the basis of cosmic order. If people stayed in harmony with sound then they would live harmoniously together. Emperors understood the need to maintain this harmony. As a result, the emperor and even wealthy noblemen retained large troops of dancers and musicians. Early thinkers believed music had moral powers, and Confucius (551–479 B.C.E.) thought music was nearly as important as food. He believed different kinds of music had different properties. By playing an instrument, singing, or listening to music, Confucius

This nineteenth-century illustration shows a Chinese man and his servant. He is playing a *qin*, or Chinese zither, one of the most popular instruments in China. It is still played today.

believed an inner state of harmony could be achieved. However, certain types of music, he thought, might encourage bad behavior. For example, he considered the ancient Shao dance to have a positive influence by bringing harmony, while the music of the Zheng (*Jung*) region, which lies just south of his home state of Lu, he claimed was dangerous, encouraging bad ideas. "Get rid of the tunes of Zheng," he is quoted as saying. "The tunes of Zheng are lascivious."

Another influential Confucian thinker was Xunzi (*Shoo'un-tzuh*) or Master Xun (c. 310–c. 220 B.C.E.), who collected his ideas in a set of essays. At this time, books were known by the name of their author only, so this set is known as the *Xunzi*. Xunzi made a connection between "music" and "pleasure" because both are written with the same character. Xunzi argued that music equaled joy and the enjoyment of music affected people of all social classes. As such, a ruler could use music to maintain order and harmony among his subjects.

The pitch and sound of music were also considered important. Cosmological theorists studied the relationship between pitch measurements and numbers. They were also eager to interpret sound and its relationship to other natural phenomena. Music was a very important part of court ceremonies, and bronze bells found in the tombs of noblemen testify to this. During the rule of Emperor Wu Di (*Woo-dee*) (156–87 B.C.E.) of the Han Dynasty, a *Yuefu* (office of music) was created. Its role was to collect popular ballads and music as well as organizing musical performances at court and for military occasions. By the time the office was abolished in 7 B.C.E., it employed 830 musicians, players, singers, acrobats, and dancers. While this seems a large number, it is small compared with the 30,000 imperial employees of the Tang

This dancing figure was carved from jade and dates from the Warring States Period (475–221 B.C.E.).

The Chinese System of Musical Notation

In Chinese music there were five pitches (*wusheng*), and twelve half tones (*lülü*). The half tones were based on the sounds made by bamboo pipes (*lü*), which, according to legend, were introduced by the mythological Yellow Emperor, Huang Di.

Dynasty (618-907 C.E.) who were responsible for organizing court music and dances during the reign of Emperor Xuanzong (*Shoo'ann-tzong*), who ruled 712–756 C.E. During his reign, a particular kind of music known as *yanyue* (enjoyable music) was popular at court.

Performances, however, were not confined to the court. Ordinary people in ancient China enjoyed performing and listening to music, and dancing was particularly popular.

Chinese Opera

Performances of various forms of music, dance, and acrobatics held an important position in traditional Chinese life and were considered to be one way of communicating with ancestral spirits as well as an effective way of expressing feelings. The power of the state was reflected in the theatrical performances. Eventually all these different art forms had merged together to evolve into a distinct national music-drama that bears some similarities to certain types of opera in the West.

During the Tang Dynasty a type of performance called *canjunxi* (*tsan-joo'un-shee*) ("adjutant plays"; an adjutant was a military rank) emerged. In a *canjunxi* show, two actors, who were usually men, performed comic dialogues accompanied by string, wind, and percussion instruments. As an urban middle class emerged during the Song Dynasty (960-1279 C.E.), the popularity of the performing arts grew rapidly. Two art forms emerged in north and south China, the *zaju* (variety play) and *nanxi* (*nan-shee*) (southern theater). A typical *zaju* show combined music with dancing, acting, and acrobatics.

During the rule of the Mongol emperors of the Yuan Dynasty and particularly under Kublai Khan, who ruled from 1260 to 1294 C.E., north and south China were reunited and *zaju* became the most important artistic form of entertainment. Most of the performances were comprised of four acts with the main character singing throughout the whole performance. No musical scores from this time survive, but paintings show that musicians playing flutes and drums, and people clapping their hands, often accompanied the shows. As the Yuan Dynasty came to an end, southern drama revived and during the sixteenth century a form of opera, known as *kunqu* (*koo'un-choo*), emerged in a town close to Shanghai. The music of these operas was set to literary texts, and they were very long, with as many as fifty scenes performed over a

This mural, painted on the wall of a temple in Shanxi province during the Ming Dynasty (1368–1644 C.E.), shows the end of a performance of a Yuan Dynasty (1279–1368 C.E.) poetic drama.

number of days. The themes were often sad. Kunqu spread across China around the end of the seventeenth century when scholar-officials, who often took actors with them on their official postings, started to watch it.

Court Orchestras

Many court occasions were accompanied by music, so the court orchestras were kept very busy. When the emperor received dignitaries, entertained, or wanted to be entertained, he called upon his orchestra to provide music. The musicians were often women, dressed in their court finery, and the most common instruments were wind and string instruments. They played the *sheng* (flute) and the *qin* (*chin*) (zither). Another popular instrument the musicians played was the drum.

During the Tang Dynasty (618–907 C.E.), court banquet orchestras were very popular even as far away as in neighboring Korea and Japan. Orchestras from across Asia were invited to perform in the court and many of them became a regular part of entertainment during the Tang Dynasty. The jade chime and bronze bell, often found in the tombs of important people, were frequently added to the court orchestras to give a ceremonial quality to the performance. During the Song Dynasty (960–1279 C.E.), court orchestras lost popularity to the opera and local musicals.

Types of Instruments

The ancient Chinese played a large variety of instruments. These are still part of traditional Chinese orchestras today.

Sheng

The *sheng* is a kind of mouth organ made from bamboo pipes. An orchestra would feature several *sheng* played at the same time.

This painting is part of a horizontal scroll called "Han Xizai Gives a Night Party," painted by Gu Hongzhong (937–975 C.E.). Note the female musicians performing for Han Xizai (center).

Qin

The *qin*, a Chinese zither, is at least 2,000 years old. The older zithers had more strings, while more recent ones had fewer strings stretched over a long, slightly curved body. The *qin* looks a little bit like a guitar or fiddle but does not have a neck protruding from the body. It was one of the most popular of all the ancient Chinese instruments. Its distinctive sound, almost like a plaintive cry, formed much of the ancient music.

Xiao

The earliest *xiao* (flute) is one of the world's oldest instruments, dating back more than 7,000 years. It was made from bone. Later *xiao* were made from bamboo, which meant that they were affordable by ordinary people and not just for court musicians.

Pipa or Ruan

Another very old instrument, the earliest *pipa* or lute, also known as *ruan*, was made during the Qin Dynasty (221–206 B.C.E.) and is the Chinese equivalent of a guitar. It reached the peak of its popularity during the Tang Dynasty (618–907 C.E.). Named after a fruit, the *pipa* was played by everyone from court musicians to local people. Its body was shaped like a pear, and it had four strings. There was a smaller version of the *pipa* known as the *liuqin* (*lee'oh-chin*), which sounded similar to a mandolin.

Musicians in Tombs

Since music was considered an integral part of daily life, it followed that musical instruments were placed in tombs. In early China groups of musicians were put to death and their bodies buried alongside the deceased so they could play for them in the afterlife. Sets of instruments used in court performances have been found in tombs from the Western and Eastern Zhou (*Joe*) dynasties (1050–221 B.C.E.). The instruments included stone chimes, bronze drums, string instruments similar to lutes, bamboo flutes, and bells. Female painted terracotta figures playing the harp, flute, and lute have been found in tombs from the Tang Dynasty. Often, a terracotta dancer was placed with the musicians.

Dance

Traditional Chinese dance was, like music, an important part of daily life. Dance grew out of ritual activities such as the worship of ancestors. In ancient China, professional sorcerers performed dances. It was believed that ritual dances could end droughts, bring rain, or even stop

500 B.C.E.	Qin Dynasty 221–206 B.C.E.		I C.E.		
Eastern Zhou Dynasty 770–221 B.C.E.			Han Dynasty 206 B.C.E.–220 C.E.		Period of Disunity
Confucius 551–479 C.E.	Marquis Yi tomb	Xunzi c.300–230 B.C.E.	Yuefu (Office of Music) created		

This bronze drum dates from the early Shang Dynasty (c. 1600–1050 B.C.E.). Musical instruments were placed in tombs to be played by the dead person's personal musicians, who would sometimes be killed and buried alongside them.

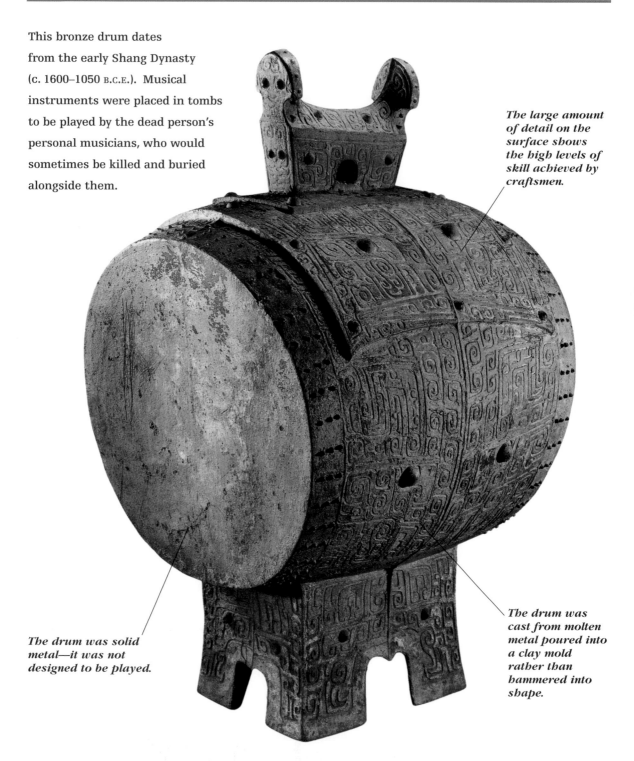

The large amount of detail on the surface shows the high levels of skill achieved by craftsmen.

The drum was solid metal—it was not designed to be played.

The drum was cast from molten metal poured into a clay mold rather than hammered into shape.

Sui Dynasty 589–618 C.E.	1000 C.E.		1500 C.E.
Tang Dynasty 618–907 C.E.	Song Dynasty 960–1279 C.E.	Yuan Dynasty 1279–1368 C.E.	Ming Dynasty 1368–1644 C.E.
The Drunken Concubine 745–755 C.E.	*Zaju* (variety plays) popular		*Kunqu* opera popular

This stone carved figure is of a female musician playing the lute. It dates from 595 C.E. and was discovered in the tomb of General Zhang Sheng of the Sui Dynasty (589–618 C.E.).

evil spirits. Dance also became a part of political ceremony as well as a form of entertainment. In the first millennium B.C.E., a scholar wrote in the *Shijing* (Classic of Poetry), one of the landmark books of Confucianism, that dance was a means of expressing feelings when words were not enough. "Feelings arise within us," he wrote, "and may be expressed in the form of words. If words alone do not suffice to express our feelings, we sigh. If sighing fails, we sing. If singing is still not enough, we express them by dancing with our hands and feet."

The *Shijing* gave descriptions of different dances used during the Western and Eastern Zhou dynasties (1050–221 B.C.E.). During this time, dance was part of the education of noblemen and it was believed that when a man could dance it showed he had reached a balance between his mind and body. Later, during the Tang Dynasty, the influence of other Asian cultures became apparent in China. These dances became part of new local dances. The Tang emperor Xuanzong, who ruled from 712 to 756 C.E., founded a court academy of dance and

An Old Orchestra

Archaeologists made an amazing discovery in 1978. Excavating the tomb of Marquis Yi of Zeng, who lived during the fifth century B.C.E., they uncovered a complete ritual orchestra. The discovery provided a unique insight into Chinese music of 2,400 years ago. His tomb contained 124 instruments including drums, flutes, mouth organs, panpipes, large *se* zithers, small *qin* zithers, 32 chime stones, and a 64-piece bronze bell set complete with stands.

The bells and chime stones can still be played. The bronze bells have inscriptions that give their pitches and also indicate that they were presented as gifts. They are fine examples of bell casting and offer evidence that bell making had reached a high level. The large zithers have around 25 strings while the small zithers have just 5 strings. All the zithers are slightly different, suggesting they may have come from different parts of the state and were used to perform regional music.

Chime stones and bells were used to make what was known as "suspended music," which was unique to Chinese music. The chime stones were played to start and end a performance and were used to tune the rest of the orchestra. The bells were made of bronze, and originated in southern China. During the Western Zhou Dynasty (c. 1050–771 B.C.E.), the bells were imported into the Zhou capital and neighboring area (present-day Shaanxi province) and they also appeared in northern China, and were a crucial part of Zhou court music.

The bronze bells discovered in the tomb of the Marquis Yi of Zeng are a range of different sizes and make up the largest bronze musical instrument ever uncovered by archaeologists.

music called *Liyuan* (The Pear Garden). The emperor himself took part in the training and rehearsal of musicians and dancers at the academy.

Dance was not just limited to the court. Dancers in certain parts of the capital performed for the public. Paintings from the time of the Tang Dynasty (618–907 C.E.) show dancers wearing long skirts that swirled as they performed, adding to the effect of the dance. Tang poets wrote poems to celebrate the dancing, and as theater became more important in later ancient China, dance became a central part of theatrical shows.

These bronze dancers were made during the Han Dynasty (206 B.C.E.–220 C.E.).

Whirling Dance

During the seventh and eighth centuries, a kind of dance, known as the "whirling dance" became very popular in China. Sogdian girls from Central Asian cities such as Samarkand were the original performers of this kind of dance. They wore clothing in shades of crimson and green, and twirled around on small circular rugs, accompanied by music. Yang Guifei (*Yang-gweh-fey*) (719–756 C.E.), who was the favorite

concubine (secondary wife) of one of the Tang emperors, took lessons in this dance in the palace in Chang'an (Xi'an in Shaanxi province). The dance was thought to be almost verging on the indecent compared with the more sedate Chinese dances that were common at the time.

The whirling dance is portrayed in this mural from the Mogao caves at Dunhuang in northwest China. The painting dates from the Tang Dynasty (618–907 C.E.).

Chinese Opera

The many popular Chinese operas performed today have their roots in ancient Chinese operas. One opera, *The Drunken Concubine*, dates from around 745–755 C.E. The story follows the Emperor Xuanzong's favorite concubine (one of the emperor's secondary wives) named Yang Guifei. Over the course of one evening we see her mood shift from one of joy to anger to jealousy to drunken playfulness and finally a sense of defeat and resignation.

One evening, the emperor arranges to meet Yang Guifei in a pavilion in the imperial gardens. She prepares a banquet for him and sits awaiting his arrival after he has finished his imperial duties. The emperor does not appear. Instead, he has gone to visit another concubine. After Yang Guifei is told where the emperor has gone, she gets angry and decides to eat the food alone. She demands an alcoholic drink, and, as she drinks more and more, the audience watches her mood change.

Yang Guifei tries to pretend she is not drunk but it soon becomes clear that she is. She refuses help from the servants and when she cannot walk her maids have to support her. The servants are worried she will ask for more alcohol, and to keep her quiet they pretend the emperor is coming. When she realizes this is a lie, Yang Guifei gets angry again and orders a servant to tell the emperor to come. When the servant refuses, she slaps his cheek. Then, she removes his hat and puts it on her head, pretending to walk like a man before throwing the hat back at the servant. Finally, the servants persuade her to return to her rooms and she stumbles away, supported by her maids.

Two of the most famous figures from Chinese opera, the Emperor Xuanzong and his favorite concubine Yang Guifei, are illustrated here in embroidered and decorated silk.

Chapter Four

Houses and Public Buildings

Chinese architecture is mainly wooden and, since early times, has relied on a strict principle based on a wooden frame that carries the load of the roof without any help from the walls. There are two forms of houses, the *yin* and the *yang*. *Yin* houses are tombs built for the dead, and these are made from more durable stone and brick. The *yang* home, traditionally made of wood, is for the living.

Over the centuries, Chinese architecture has followed these principles and has changed little, except in the details. Buildings have maintained their distinctive shape and the alterations have largely been decorative. In domestic architecture, a home reflected status and anyone who could afford to build their own home did so. Imperial architecture was about impressing the masses with splendor and opulence. The large halls, with their overhanging tiled roofs and hundreds of subsidiary buildings, reflected the power of the emperor. Religious temples were built on the same principle and design. Imperial, religious, domestic, and tomb architecture was built according to the principles of *Feng Shui* (*Fung-shoo'eh*).

The most magnificent example of imperial architecture is the Forbidden City in Beijing. Home to fourteen emperors between 1368 and 1912, the palaces and halls of the Forbidden City illustrate the many important principles of Chinese architecture.

At the heart of the Forbidden City in Beijing, once home to fourteen emperors, is the Golden Bell Hall, also known as the Hall of Supreme Harmony. It is one of three great halls in the Forbidden City.

Since buildings were made of wood, most of the early ones have not survived. The oldest wooden building in China dates from the Tang Dynasty (618–907 C.E.). However, pottery models of traditional homes, which were buried with the dead, give us a good idea of how the architecture evolved. Tombs built of more lasting materials have survived and also tell us much about Chinese architecture. Garden design also played a central role in the planning of homes, temples, palaces, and Chinese cities.

Features of Chinese Architecture

Some of the earliest people living in southeastern China in Zheijang province built homes using interlocking pieces of wood. There, archaeologists have discovered wood that is more than 6,500 years old. During China's Bronze Age (c. 2000–771 B.C.E.), building complexes featuring more than one courtyard, arcades, and connecting causeways were also built entirely out of wood. The advantage of wood in climates as diverse as those of China is its ability to expand and contract according to the weather conditions.

Chinese builders used a system of counting the gaps between wooden columns, which supported the roof, to give the overall size of the dwelling. A typical house consisted of three gaps, known as *jian* (bays). The advantage of this system of building is that a house could be expanded as children were born or the family grew wealthier. This system was also used in imperial and religious buildings. Outer walls were sometimes made of brick or lighter bamboo wattle, and plastered with clay or pounded earth. Inner walls were often plastered and painted.

The most distinctive feature of a traditional Chinese building is the roof. Tiled roofs sat on top of the wooden columns supported on a series of wooden brackets. The wooden brackets added extra reinforcement to the roofs, which traditionally hung over the structure. The number of wooden brackets and the complexity of the roof reflected the wealth of the owner. In the Han Dynasty (206 B.C.E.–220 C.E.) and before, roofs just sloped. But beginning in the fifth century they showed an inner curve that became more pronounced, especially in southern China. The overhanging tiled roofs had two main uses. They allowed rain to run off and, during the hot summers, gave protection from the sun. Once the wooden columns were erected, the walls and internal partitions were made from interwoven materials—such as bamboo or branches and plaster. Sidewalls were not built to bear weight so they could easily be replaced when the owner wanted to make the house bigger. The building and main entrance always faced south, according to the principles of *Feng Shui.*

Houses built of stone and brick were more common in southern China, where wood was not as readily available. In southern China, adobe bricks made of sun-dried earth and straw were prepared all year round. Stone was not a popular building material, however, because it was considered "unnatural."

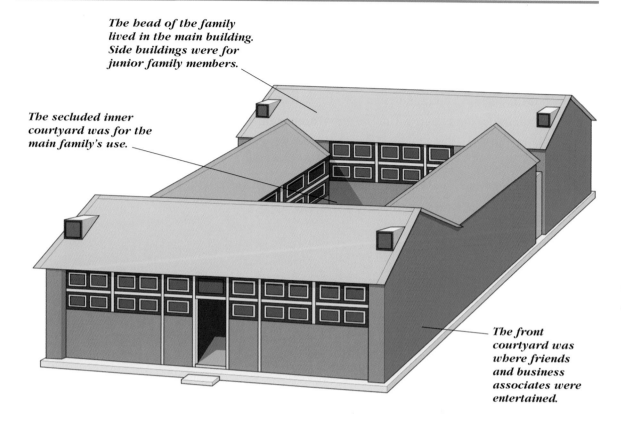

The head of the family lived in the main building. Side buildings were for junior family members.

The secluded inner courtyard was for the main family's use.

The front courtyard was where friends and business associates were entertained.

This is an example of a typical Chinese courtyard house. Over succeeding dynasties the houses became more complex but the basic layout remained the same.

The courtyard house was the typical Chinese dwelling and most were single story, but might have included a two-story reception hall.

Feng Shui

The building of any Chinese structure had to take into account the Chinese belief system of *Feng Shui*. By following the rules of *Feng Shui*, the Chinese believed they were helping to ensure that their chosen site was in harmony with the fundamental principles of nature so that it would be as auspicious (favorable) as possible. The site had to make the best use of the natural environment, including the mountains and valleys. From the time of the earliest civilizations, the Chinese have always tried to position their

Straight Walking Spirits

Look in the front gate of a courtyard house and you will only see a screen. This was to retain the privacy of the family in their courtyard but also had another function: to deter evil spirits. The ancient Chinese believed that spirits can only walk in straight lines, so the screen would prevent them from entering the house.

structures on a north–south axis. This was also the case with tombs. If possible, it was most auspicious to place a tomb on a hillside facing south. Another important factor was the timing of the construction. Not only were certain days considered lucky or unlucky, but also certain hours. Certain colors, such as red, blue, and yellow, were considered lucky. Symmetry was also crucial in the construction of any Chinese building. The entrance had to balance either side of the front façade. Access to the sky was considered vital. Even the smallest

Rich Chinese landowners could afford to build multi-storied houses with several courtyards in the best *Feng Shui* position, facing south on a hillside.

house in a city would have some place that was open to the sky, which was known as the "Well of Heaven." Similarly, some plants and the presence of water, to balance nature and to reflect the clouds, were also important.

Family Houses

In ancient China, it was usual for more than one generation of a family to live together in the same house. Grandparents, parents, and children often shared a home. There were strict rules about how they lived and this was reflected in the way the house was organized. The typical courtyard home was divided into different sections. The inner or rear courtyard was where the

family lived with the head of the house, usually the grandfather and his immediate family, in the main building. Other close relatives lived in the side rooms. Within the main building there was a special place where the family kept their ancestral tablets. The household shrine was where the family sought advice from their ancestors and where they paid respects to their ancestors on one of the many specially designated days throughout the year.

Domestic architecture is the oldest continuing building tradition in China. Houses in ancient China shared many common features that have changed little over centuries. For example, houses were always built to face south to shelter them from the strong winds that came down

Pottery Houses

Because most Chinese houses were made principally from wood, there are no remains of structures from the Qin (221–206 B.C.E.) or Han (206 B.C.E.–220 C.E.) dynasties. However, we still know a lot about how these ancient homes were designed from pottery models that have survived in tombs. The tombs often also contain pottery models of the human and animal inhabitants of the house, as well as some of the furniture. Sketches of houses and their layout were also drawn on the walls of tombs. The tombs themselves were built like underground houses.

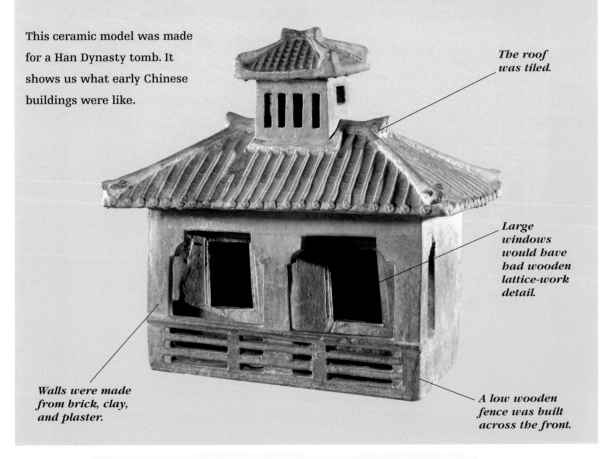

This ceramic model was made for a Han Dynasty tomb. It shows us what early Chinese buildings were like.

The roof was tiled.

Large windows would have had wooden lattice-work detail.

Walls were made from brick, clay, and plaster.

A low wooden fence was built across the front.

Pavilions

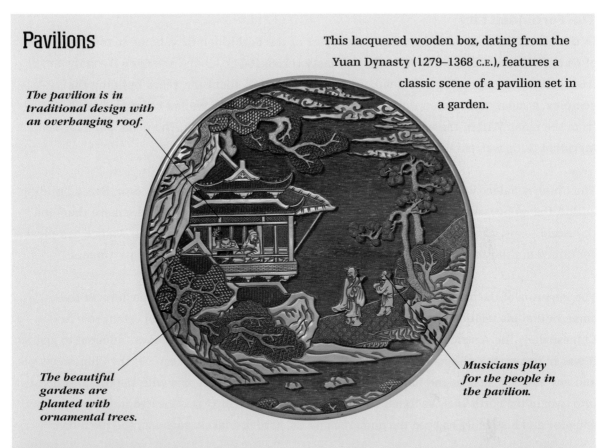

The pavilion is in traditional design with an overhanging roof.

This lacquered wooden box, dating from the Yuan Dynasty (1279–1368 C.E.), features a classic scene of a pavilion set in a garden.

The beautiful gardens are planted with ornamental trees.

Musicians play for the people in the pavilion.

Pavilions are among the most characteristic sights seen across China. They are small, distinctive buildings that serve many different functions, including a place for relaxation and contemplation, and are situated to provide scenic views both in and outside gardens. Pavilions have an overhanging tiled roof and open windows that allow the visitor to sit and contemplate the view. There is a saying in China, "There is no famous mountain without a pavilion, no rivers or lakes without pavilions, and no parks or gardens without pavilions." The pavilion has been an essential component of any Chinese park or garden since the early days of ancient China. The great variety of designs and styles of pavilions are a reflection of the Chinese culture. Pavilions take up little space and come in many styles, so they are easy and inexpensive to build. However, the decision to build, the choice of a site, the naming of the pavilion, and the sayings that were carved on the pavilion all reveal much about the spiritual goals of the builder.

from the north and to agree with *Feng Shui* principles. Homes, no matter how big or small, were built using the system of bays, and a typical house was three bays wide. Richer families might build their homes with five bays. However many bays there were, there were always an odd number of them, because even numbers were considered unlucky. Domestic houses were built on the same structural principles as larger temples and palaces, with a wooden structure supporting the roof and walls that did not bear weight. There are differences in style and materials between different regions of China and at different periods in Chinese history.

The Forbidden City

In the heart of Beijing lies the massive complex of the Forbidden City, home to fourteen rulers of China's last two dynasties, the Ming Dynasty (1368–1644 C.E.) and the Qing Dynasty (1644–1911 C.E.). According to legend, one million workers spent ten years building the complex. A moat surrounded the Forbidden City and numerous walled courtyards radiated from the moat. Within the walls, every terrace and gate faced south. The principal gate, the Meridian Gate, was particularly magnificent.

The Chinese palace was the symbol of the power and authority of the emperor. Every building within the palace complex—and in the case of the Forbidden City there were more than one thousand—was arranged and positioned to reflect the power of the emperor. Palace complexes contained similar features such as the emperor's throne room and private apartments.

The intention of the magnificent palace complex was to reflect the elevated position of the emperor and his relationship with the cosmic forces that played such an important role in Chinese daily life. A strict hierarchy in the position of the palace buildings was adhered to just as it was in domestic architecture. A high wall surrounded the palace to keep out the Chinese people and any enemies. Rooms and halls were arranged on a north–south axis with the complex divided into two: in the north was the "inner court" while the "outer court" was located in the south. The emperor and his family enjoyed the numerous parks, gardens, lakes, pagodas, and pavilions.

Imperial Architecture

The Chinese dragon was an emblem reserved for the exclusive use of the imperial family. It was widely used on imperial buildings. Dragons appeared on roofs, beams, pillars, and doors. Only buildings used by the imperial family were allowed to have nine *jian* (bays). The emperor's gates were the only ones that could have five arches above the gate, with the central arch being reserved for the exclusive use of the emperor. The imperial buildings favored red walls and yellow-tiled roofs, as used in the buildings of the Forbidden City.

This decorated yellow roof tile was for use only on the emperor's buildings. Yellow was used exclusively for the imperial family. The dragon's association with the emperor dates from the time of the First Emperor Qin (259–210 B.C.E.), who made the dragon his emblem.

The inner court was home to the emperor, the empress, and his other consorts, as well as his closest advisors and guards. In the outer court were the offices of the ministries and government officials. The emperor greeted foreign guests in one of the many ceremonial halls, often the Hall of Supreme Harmony, where he sat on his dragon throne, while large ceremonies and parades were held in the courtyards of the outer palace.

The Forbidden City was planned and designed according to the principles of *Feng Shui*. A river that ran south of the main palace with five bridges crossing it bisected the first court.

The Palace-Cities

The large, centralized structures built by the earliest Chinese rulers served as models for the later palace architecture. During the Eastern Zhou Dynasty (770–221 B.C.E.), each ruler's city had its own palace complex, but after First Emperor Qin (259–210 B.C.E.) unified China in 221 B.C.E., the emperors built more than one capital. As bureaucracy grew, the palace complexes were built to a standard plan so the court could move from one capital to another with minimal disruption.

The emperors of the Sui Dynasty (589–618 C.E.) and the Tang Dynasty (618–907 C.E.) built palace-cities in their principal capitals, Chang'an and Luoyang. Taizong (599–649 C.E.), the Tang emperor who ruled from 626 to 649 C.E., started work on his palace in 634. It was typical of the imperial residences of the seventh to ninth centuries, with the buildings laid out in a "U" shape. The Tang emperors also had palaces in other cities, which they used when they were away from the imperial capital.

There are few remains of the palace-cities of the Song Dynasty (960–1279 C.E.), although written records suggest they were magnificent. The Mongol ruler Kublai Khan (1215–1294 C.E.), built his palace in Dadu (present-day Beijing) according to classical principles of Chinese architecture partly in an attempt to legitimize Mongol rule in China. The best surviving example of a palace-city is still the Forbidden City.

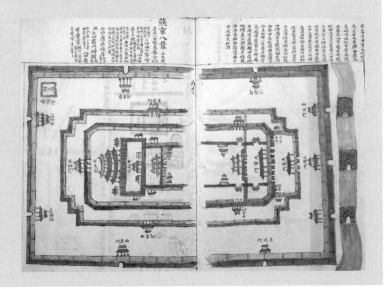

This eighteenth-century Vietnamese map clearly shows the moat that surrounds the Forbidden City in Beijing.

This illustration shows an overview of part of the Forbidden City in Beijing. Within its walls were more than 8,000 rooms. No ordinary person was allowed to enter the city—only the emperor, his family, his servants, and officials.

Images of dragons decorate the entire complex. On the side of the marble stairs are carved dragons. The dragon was the sign of the emperor while the phoenix was the sign of the empress. There are many carvings of the phoenix throughout the Forbidden City.

In the Hall of Preserving Harmony, the emperor sometimes put on his imperial robes before being carried in his sedan chair to the Hall of Supreme Harmony. It was also used for banquets and as an examination hall.

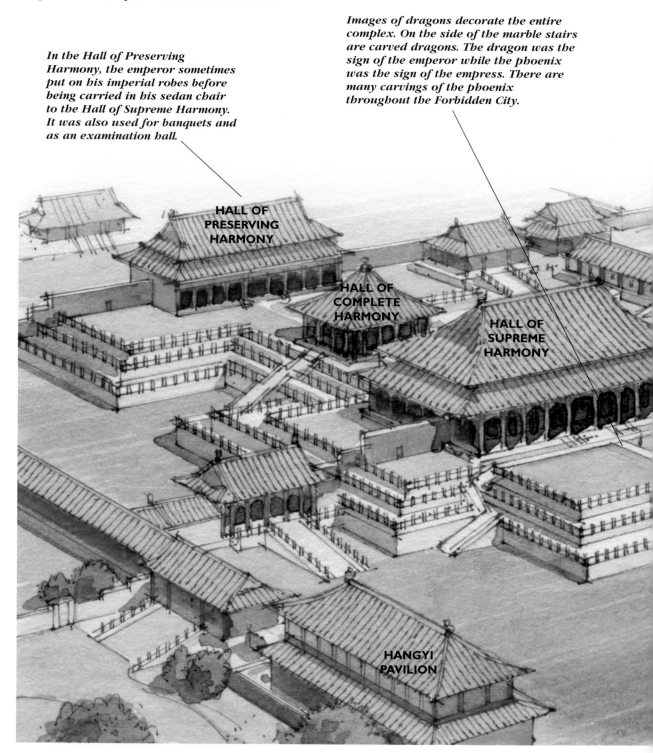

HALL OF PRESERVING HARMONY

HALL OF COMPLETE HARMONY

HALL OF SUPREME HARMONY

HANGYI PAVILION

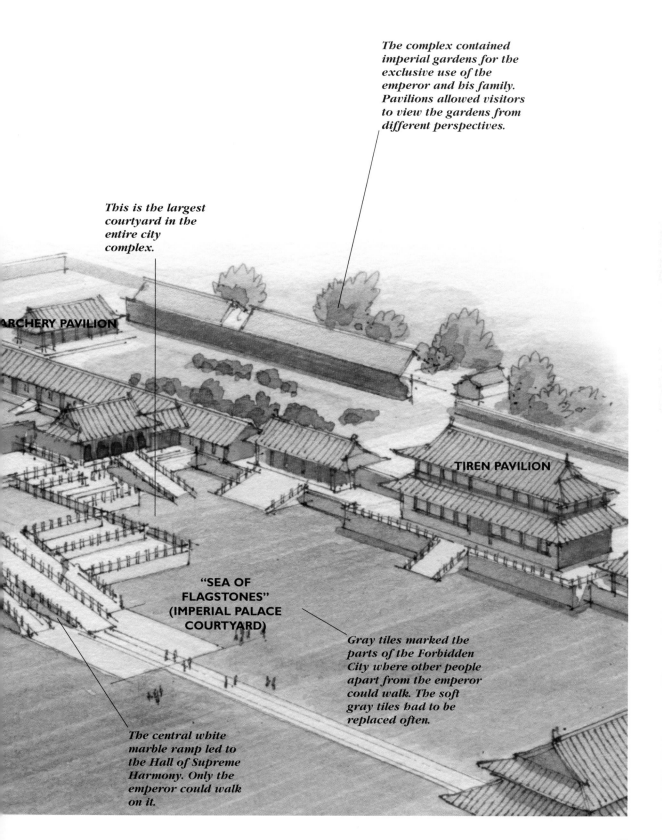

The complex contained imperial gardens for the exclusive use of the emperor and his family. Pavilions allowed visitors to view the gardens from different perspectives.

This is the largest courtyard in the entire city complex.

ARCHERY PAVILION

TIREN PAVILION

"SEA OF FLAGSTONES" (IMPERIAL PALACE COURTYARD)

Gray tiles marked the parts of the Forbidden City where other people apart from the emperor could walk. The soft gray tiles had to be replaced often.

The central white marble ramp led to the Hall of Supreme Harmony. Only the emperor could walk on it.

Chapter Five

Tombs and Temples

Some of the most important groups of buildings, or complexes, were religious in origin. The Chinese *miao* (temple) or *si* (monastery) consisted of a number of buildings. From outside, these complexes looked very similar to imperial palace complexes. In ancient China, religious complexes were built by followers of three different belief systems: Buddhism, Daoism, and Confucianism.

Confucianism and Daoism both appeared about the same time, during the fifth century B.C.E. Buddhism came to China from India during the Han Dynasty (206 B.C.E.–220 C.E.) and grew to become a major religion. Although it is convenient to refer to them as religions, neither Confucianism nor Daoism started off as a religion. However, Confucianism and Daoism became linked with Buddhism, and their followers started to build monasteries and temples following the Buddhist model.

The imperial court was organized around a strong religious faith. The emperor and the court shamans were believed to hold *de* (magical power), and were the only ones who could communicate directly with the spirits of the afterlife. In order to keep the spirits of ancestors and the gods of nature happy, it was essential to perform complicated rituals that required lots of equipment, which was housed in temples.

Though the temples were designed for different belief systems, they shared certain common features, and provided the setting for rituals from the earliest days of

The Emperor Shao Hao's tomb is the only pyramid-shaped tomb of a Chinese emperor. It dates from the Song Dynasty (960–1279 C.E.) and is located in Qufu, Shandong province.

Large Monastery Complexes

Few temples survive from before the tenth century C.E. However, from archaeological excavations and written records we do know that following the introduction of Buddhism into China, large monastery complexes were built. They normally consisted of vast enclosed complexes with many courtyards and hundreds of buildings. The appearance and layout of the monasteries were heavily influenced by palace architecture. The emperor's throne room was transformed into the chief worship hall with the main Buddha image at its center.

ancient Chinese civilization. Daoists believed that the natural world, especially a mountain, was the spiritual home of the immortals. Daoist hermits retreated to live, pray, and contemplate in the countryside and mountaintops. They felt that higher places were better, because they felt nearer to the immortals. The Confucians, in contrast, believed in an ordered society that was based on the strictly hierarchical court life. For them, temples in an urban setting were suitable places to worship, because they did not worship nature like the Daoists.

Across China, Buddhists built cave temples, as they had originally done in India. Caves offer natural protection, which is why many examples have survived across China dating from as early as the fourth century C.E. The temples were carved straight into the rock face and then filled with sculptures and pictures of the Buddha, *bodhisattvas* (people who had reached the Buddhist state of enlightenment but stayed on earth to help others), and various gods.

The Longxing (*Long-shing*) monastery in Zhengding (*Jung-ding*), in Hebei (*Huh-bay*) province, is typical of Buddhist temple complexes built between the ninth and fourteenth centuries. Constructed from wood, it is made up of a number of halls positioned north to south. In addition to the prayer halls, the monks lived and ate in the complex so their accommodations are located on the east side of the complex. Daoist complexes were also laid out in a similar fashion, with prayer halls and living space for the monks contained within the complex. One of the most spectacular was Yonglegong, which was built during the thirteenth century.

Magnificent Cave Temples

The cave temples in Dunhuang, in the remote Gansu province, date from the fourth century C.E. and are some of the most magnificent examples of Buddhist temples. There were perhaps as many as 1,000 temples originally carved out of the cliffs. Today, 492 caves survive and within them are painted walls, which show, among other things, stories from the Buddha's life. Statues of the Buddha, in many different poses, were also sculpted in many of the caves.

This fifth-century cave at Dunhuang features several painted clay statues, such as the one shown here. The painting on the wall behind forms part of the same composition.

Buddhist Temples

After Buddhism arrived from India, it spread rapidly and reached its peak during the first two centuries of the Tang Dynasty (618–907 C.E.). But Buddhism suffered a setback around 843 C.E. when the Tang Emperor Wuzong (814–846 C.E.) turned against China's religions, particularly Buddhism, and ordered the destruction of thousands of temples and monasteries.

As well as pioneering cave temples, the Buddhists also built freestanding temples and monasteries. Those built before the Ming Dynasty (1368–1644 C.E.) were constructed of wood and some survive to this day. The Southern Zen Temple (Nanchansi), in the Wutai Mountains in Shaanxi province, was built in 782 C.E. and is the oldest wooden building that still stands in China. It probably survived the persecution during the Tang Dynasty (618–907 C.E.) because it is very remote. It is a perfect example of the Chinese style of Buddhist temple, with a three-bay hall and a spectacular roof with projecting eaves. Its gentle sloping roof marked a change from the temple architecture of the Sui

The Buddhist Way of Life

Buddhists had introduced to China a new way of living and praying. Buddhist monks and nuns lived and prayed in separate religious complexes, which housed temples and all necessary additional buildings. This system of separate lives for religious men and women went against the basic Chinese belief—stressed by Confucius—that one's responsibility to family and society was to have children.

This ornately carved jade Buddhist figure is displayed in Nanchan Monastery at Mount Wutai, which was built in 782 C.E.

Dynasty (589–618 C.E.). On the top of the roof are two *chiwei* (owl tails). The ornaments curl toward each other and were supposed to represent a mythical sea monster that gave protection against fire. Inside the hall are seventeen painted clay statues, from the time of the Tang, positioned around a central Buddha.

Daoist Temples

Unlike Buddhism, Daoism originally did not have any images of its gods. It was not until the Tang Dynasty (618–907 C.E.) that large stone sculptures were carved. One surviving Daoist temple is the Qingyang gong (*Ching-yang-gong*) (Green Sheep Hall) in Chengdu, capital of Sichuan (*Suh-choo'ann*) province. It is one of the most famous of all Chinese temples and was founded during the Tang Dynasty. The surviving buildings, however, date from the Qing Dynasty (1644–1911 C.E.). The most magnificent building of the complex is the Eight Trigrams Pavilion. Built on square foundations, it has a colored, glazed dome on top. It is octagonal in shape to reflect the ancient Chinese philosophy that "the sky is round and the

The Buddha

The different Buddhist temples housed one or more images of the Buddha, whose name means "enlightened one." Buddha (c. 563–c. 483 B.C.E.) was a prince from northern India who spent his life searching for personal peace or enlightenment. He believed that if he gave up worldly desires, such as expensive clothes and fine food, he might reach a state known as *nirvana*, where the self ceases to exist and is thus free from all the worries and upsets of the everyday world. When his followers built temples to house the images of the Buddha, they used hundreds of different poses of him sitting, reclining, or standing.

This is the largest Buddha figure in the world, known as the Lingyun Buddha. It was carved between 713 and 803 C.E. and is over 200 feet (71 meters) high.

A Daoist nun prepares an altar table before a ceremony in the Qingyang gong (Green Sheep Hall) in Chengdu, Sichuan province.

earth is square." There are eight pillars with dragons drawn in relief in the corridor. Overhead are *caissons* (domed or coffered ceilings) with ornate symbols of eight trigrams arranged across them.

Confucian Temples

One of the most important buildings in China is located in the town of Qufu (*Choo-foo*) in Shandong province. It is the Temple of Confucius, and is the largest of all the Confucian temples. A philosopher and wise man, Confucius (551–479 B.C.E.), was born and died in Qufu. The temple was established in 478 B.C.E., just one year after his death. Confucius stressed the need for sound, moral government and for citizens to be dutiful and honorable, especially in their behavior toward the elderly. His ideas have had a huge influence on China that continues to this day. The Confucian temples reflect the significant position Confucius held in Chinese society and their style influenced Eastern architecture across the region.

Confucian temples were usually built as part of a large complex, similar to the imperial complexes, and were attached to Confucian schools. Just like the Forbidden City, Confucian temple complexes are built around courtyards. Typically, there are three courtyards, though the Temple of Confucius at Qufu has nine. The principal building is located in the central courtyard and it is where the Confucius Ancestral Tablet is displayed.

Unlike Buddhist and Daoist temples, Confucian temples do not always contain images, though the very early Confucian temples did have wall paintings and some sculptures that showed images of Confucius. These were soon removed, however, because this too closely resembled Buddhist temples. Also, since no one really knew what Confucius looked like, the

The Temple of Confucius at Qufu

The first temple was built in 478 B.C.E. close to Confucius's family home. The original temple was very small, consisting of just one building with three rooms where Confucius's belongings were kept. In 539 C.E., the building was renovated and a statue of Confucius was erected. Since then, consecutive rulers have expanded and renovated the temple. To date, there have been fifteen major reconstructions, and more than thirty smaller buildings have been rebuilt.

Today, the temple is the largest of more than two thousand Confucian temples across Asia and it rivals the Forbidden City in Beijing in size. The layout of the complex was designed to concentrate on the main building and is set among trees. The intention was to create an ideal of harmony, which Confucius considered to be the pinnacle of human achievement.

More than one hundred buildings make up the temple. The complex was constructed following the principles of *Feng Shui,* with the buildings following a north-south axis and the roofs finished with yellow tiles and the walls painted red.

This temple dedicated to Confucius is now a UNESCO World Heritage Site. Located in Confucius's birthplace of Qufu, it is the largest and most important of all the Confucian temples.

sculptures of him were all different. Finally, a law was passed in 1530 C.E. that ordered all the images to be removed and replaced with inscribed wooden tablets in order to unify Confucianism.

Tombs and Stupas

Because of the Chinese belief in an afterlife, tombs were built to provide lasting homes for the dead. Tombs of the second century B.C.E. and earlier are built of heavy wooden logs, but after this they were made of stone and brick. As homes that were built underground they had to include everything the occupants would need in their afterlife. The tombs often had more than one room. Living descendants visited them regularly with offerings.

As Buddhism arrived in China from India, it brought with it a new style of building, known as a *stupa* (STOO-puh), which was a type of above-ground tomb. Stupas traditionally contained relics of the Buddha, famous Buddhist monks, or Buddhist scriptures. In ancient India stupas were placed in cave temples. In China they are often tall structures, and are used to mark the site of a temple.

By the time the stupa arrived in China, probably during the Han Dynasty (206 B.C.E.–220 C.E.), its shape had changed. It kept a circular form but it was longer and slimmer. The Chinese took their urban gate tower and combined it with the form of the stupa to produce the pagoda.

Early Chinese pagodas consisted of a number of stories, each with a roof and an overhanging eave, topped with a final roof. Every Buddhist monastery in China contained a pagoda. Some early pagodas, built before the Tang Dynasty (618–907 C.E.), were as tall as 425 feet (130 meters). Most of them were made from wood so they have not survived. The only existing examples of early pagodas, from before the fifth century, are the highly carved stone pagodas inside Buddhist cave temples.

The building of pagodas flourished during the Tang Dynasty. They were built of stone, brick, or wood, and had four sides. Smaller pagodas were built to commemorate important monks and these could have as many as eight sides. Between the tenth and twelfth centuries, every Chinese Buddhist monastery had at least one pagoda-shaped stupa, with the octagonal-shaped stupa being especially popular. In the twelfth century, Zen Buddhism became more popular. Zen Buddhists did not worship in pagodas, so fewer and fewer pagodas were built.

Underground Tombs

Our understanding of Chinese culture has been greatly increased by the current excavations and discoveries of ancient tombs over the last hundred years. The most spectacular tomb so far discovered is that of First Emperor Qin, who ruled from 221 to 210 B.C.E., and was the

The White Dagoba

During Mongol rule, a particular style of stupa, known as the *dagoba*, which originally came from Tibet, started to appear in China. The most famous example of this type of stupa was the White Dagoba at the Miaoying (*Mee'ow-ying*) monastery in Beijing. Made from white brick, this dagoba was built in 1279, under the influence of one of the advisors of Kublai Khan (1215–1294).

The spire consists of a metal parasol and spire.

The White Dagoba stands more than 150 feet (50 meters) high. It has been restored on a number of occasions and was built to house religious relics.

Above the main body are thirteen rings that decrease in size. They represent the thirteen stages through which a Buddhist must pass to attain buddhahood.

The White Dagoba, also known as the white pagoda, sits on a square base and consists of a large bulb-shaped body.

emperor who unified China. Archaeologists continue to discover tombs. One of the most recent, a 2,500-year-old tomb, was discovered in January 2007 after police stopped looters from stealing from the tomb in Jiangxi province. It is of particular interest because it contains the human remains of people who were sacrificed to accompany their master into the afterlife.

Chinese buildings were traditionally built of wood, but underground funeral chambers, which replicated the architectural styles above ground, were built of earth, brick, or stone. Tombs that were not plundered have survived. Interestingly, some of the most innovative architectural designs were used in the construction of tombs. For example, the earliest vaulting in China was built underground more than 2,000 years ago. From the first millennium B.C.E., the body of the dead person was buried beneath a mound, but the burial of the dead varied from dynasty to dynasty. Some dynasties built royal necropolises—large, elaborate tombs—while others buried their emperor in an individual site.

The tomb resembled palace architecture, with part of the tomb built above ground and enclosed by walls. Just as with buildings, the tomb was built according to the principles of *Feng Shui*. Subsidiary tombs were built so that a dead person's close relatives could be buried nearby. A so-called spirit path led the way to the tomb. The entrance doors were made of wood and stone, and led to an ornately decorated passageway that descended into the tomb.

An emperor might be buried with musical instruments, such as bronze bells and ceramic figures of musicians. Prior to the fifth century B.C.E., prisoners of war and servants were sacrificed and entombed, but this practice was gradually abandoned. Imperial tombs were built to be a continuation of daily life and so were finished as elaborately as possible, but this did not just apply to the imperial family. Rich citizens were also buried in ornate tombs and, though they had to be smaller than those of royalty, such tombs were filled with items considered necessary for the afterlife.

Spirit Paths

The approach to an imperial tomb was considered an integral part of the entire structure and so was marked accordingly. Around 2,000 years ago, the imperial tomb might be designed with a formal gateway. There were freestanding gate towers and inscribed stone slabs that recorded the deeds of the dead emperor. Later, paths to the tombs might be lined with life-sized statues of officials, exotic animals, foreigners, and imperial guards. It is believed that these statues, which were made of stone, may have been intended to guard the tomb or perhaps represent a funeral procession. Even though each imperial tomb had its own spirit path, where there were groups of tombs, such as for the Ming Dynasty (1368–1644 C.E.), one path served all the tombs.

A spirit path leads to tombs from the Tang Dynasty (618–907 C.E.). This forms part of the burial site of Emperor Gaozong, who reigned between 627 and 649 C.E.

Burying the Dead

The way in which human remains were buried was extremely important to the people of ancient China. Before the arrival of Buddhism from India, the concept of rebirth did not exist in China. Instead, the ancient Chinese made extensive and thorough preparations for the death of an important figure to assist them in the afterlife. What has been discovered in the tombs that archaeologists have excavated so far has given us some of the best information about how the ancient Chinese lived.

The walls of the tomb were painted, and much of what archaeologists know about Chinese painting comes from studying the paintings on the walls of ancient tombs. The paintings, and sometimes relief sculpture, told the story of the dead person's life. The servants of the dead person were also depicted. On the ceiling of the tombs, the sun, moon, lunar lodges (the Chinese equivalent of the constellations), and sometimes signs of the zodiac were painted.

Tomb of the Jade Princess

When Prince Liu Sheng (*Lee-oo Shun*), the son of Emperor Jingdi (188–141 B.C.E.) of the Han Dynasty died in 113 B.C.E., he and his wife, Princess Tou Wan (*Toe Wan*) were buried in an imperial tomb cut into the side of a mountain in Mancheng, in Hebei province. The tombs remained undisturbed until archaeologists discovered them in 1968. The pristine state of the tombs helped them learn much about the Han Dynasty. An entrance corridor led to a number of chambers. The first rooms were used as stables and a storeroom for a carriage, among other things. Beyond these rooms, archaeologists discovered a large central room, which was used for rituals. It contained a substantial wooden structure that had a tiled roof, beneath which were tents.

Beyond these rooms were the two burial chambers. The walls were finely carved and the rooms elegantly furnished. There was also a bathroom. In the burial chamber were the coffins of the prince and princess. While the tomb is magnificent, it is the funerary costumes that are the most remarkable. Princess Tou Wan had been buried in a suit made from 2,160 pieces of jade. (The ancient Chinese believed jade had the power to preserve the body.) The jade was sewn together with 25 ounces (700 grams) of gold thread. There was another costume for the prince. In addition to the spectacular suits, the tombs contained thousands of burial objects, including many bronze and iron objects. There was also a number of gold, silver, and jade vessels for food and wine, as well as six chariots, pottery, silk, and lacquerware.

Grave Goods

Much of what we have learned about ancient Chinese culture has come from the contents of ancient tombs. When archaeologists discovered the tomb of the Han Jade Princess, it was particularly exciting because that tomb had not been plundered and its contents gave a new understanding of life during the Han Dynasty (206 B.C.E.–220 C.E.).

Many of the items placed in the thousands of tombs have rotted away. However, the widespread use of bronze, ceramics, lacquerware, and painted scrolls, along with gold, silver, jade, and other materials which have survived, has given the archaeologists plenty of information to work with.

The Terracotta Army

In March 1974, three farmers were digging a well in a field in Lintong, near the city of Xi'an, in Shaanxi province, when they uncovered the head of a terracotta warrior figurine. They had discovered the burial chamber of the First Emperor Qin (259–210 B.C.E.).

Emperor Qin unified China and ruled his subjects through terror, and his tomb reflected this. He built an underground residence that matched his palace when he was alive. To date, an army of at least 7,000 terracotta warriors found there has been noted. Only 2,000 of these have been unearthed so far and four burial pits have been opened. The farmers found Pit Number One, while pit numbers Two and Three were discovered in 1976 and 1977, following scientific surveys. A fourth pit, which was empty, was discovered in 1995. The underground tomb complex is much larger than anybody expected, covering approximately 21 square miles (56 square kilometers).

The magnificent army consists of lifesized figures with faces that are all unique. Originally, every single one was painted in bright colors. Each face and hairstyle was

Jade was used for the burial costume of Princess Tou Wan, above, because the ancient Chinese associated jade with longevity. Burying a person with jade was thought to preserve the body.

This illustration shows the construction of the tomb of the First Emperor Qin, with its rows of terracotta warriors meant to protect him in the afterlife. The emperor ordered 700,000 men to work on the building of his tomb and contents.

The floors of the corridors were paved with small bricks. The walls were lined with wooden beams and posts and the ceiling was also made from wood.

Laborers had to dig to a depth of 15 feet (5 meters) and then remove the earth. The equivalent of around 5,500 truckloads of earth were excavated.

Once the mud was removed, the workmen had to secure the walls. They did this by using rammed earth embankments.

Four large pits were
built to house the army
of terracotta warriors.
They were located
about one mile (1.6
kilometers) east of
Emperor Qin's burial
mound, visible here on
the horizon.

Reed mats were
placed on top of
the ceiling beams.
Workmen then
spread clay on
top to stop water
from penetrating
the underground
corridors.

The warriors were
molded and then
fired in workshops
and then brought
to the site.

This carved jade elephant dates from the Shang Dynasty (c. 1600–1050 B.C.E.). It was discovered in a tomb along with many other artifacts.

modeled individually while the bodies were based on two types of legs, eight torsos, and eight heads. The army replicated Qin's army with standing and kneeling archers, soldiers, cavalrymen, and chariots. Real horses were buried alongside the emperor.

When the pits were uncovered, it became apparent that the tombs had been plundered and the ceramic figures lay smashed in hundreds of pieces. The project to reassemble the pieces and rebuild the warriors continues today. Within Pit One, at the back of the massive hall that encloses the pit, are a large number of warriors in different states of repair. The actual tomb of Emperor Qin has still not been excavated. This is because Han historians described it as containing rivers and lakes of mercury, and until scientists know whether this is true or not it is too dangerous to excavate.

The Influence of Ancient Chinese Art and Architecture

A visitor to modern China will probably see little evidence of ancient Chinese art and culture in its urban landscape. But scratch below the surface and the influence is plain to see. The design of temples remains unchanged, and if you search the streets of many cities you can find traditional courtyard houses. In Japan, too, the influence of Chinese architecture is clearly seen in many of the country's pagodas. The philosophy of *Feng Shui* is still practiced today across China in every kind of public and private building. Chinese art and crafts, including painting, calligraphy, lacquer work, and ceramics, remain highly prized today, as are the semiprecious stones, such as jade, that were so valued by the emperors.

Human Sacrifice During the Shang Dynasty

Archaeologists discovered a complex of royal tombs of Shang Dynasty kings in Anyang, Henan province, the last Shang capital city. They excavated eleven royal tombs as well as more than 1,000 other tombs. The ancient Shang believed in human sacrifice and the tombs showed how this was done.

Each royal tomb was dug on a north-south axis and was a large cross-shaped pit. People and animals were led down ramps into the tomb and sacrificed so that they could accompany the king into the afterlife. The tombs contained the bodies of captured enemy soldiers, servants, women, and chariot-drivers. The sacrificed animals included pigs, oxen, and deer. Those who had worked closely with the king were buried nearest to him. Around his body were the goods he would need in the next life, including bronze cauldrons, weapons, carved jade, bone carvings, pottery, and stone sculptures. In one tomb, archaeologists found the skeleton of a dog. They think it may have been the king's favorite pet or hunting companion.

Once the king's body was laid inside the tomb, the principal body chamber was covered with a roof. The ramps approaching the tomb were filled with bronze weapons, containers of food, and ritual vessels. The bodies of more servants and prisoners were arranged in the pit. Then earth was thrown on top of the grave. Slaves pounded each layer of earth until there was a solid mound on top of the tomb.

Human sacrifice was an important part of the funeral ceremony to show the power of the king in battle and to scare those he might meet in the next life. Many of the victims were prisoners of war. They were sometimes beheaded, with the heads laid out next to the bodies.

This bronze dagger was probably used in ritual human sacrifice during the Shang Dynasty (c. 1600–1050 B.C.E.).

Glossary of Names

Confucius Chinese thinker and philosopher whose teachings and beliefs about compassion, loyalty, respect, sincerity, justice, and the ideal behavior of individuals, family, government, and society as a whole form the basis of Confucianism

Gaozong third emperor of the Tang Dynasty

Gu Hongzhong painter during the Five Dynasties era, thought to have been a court painter for Emperor Li Yu of the Tang Dynasty

Guo Xi famous landscape painter during the Song Dynasty and one of its most important artists

Han Xizai official at the court of Emperor Li Yu, who ruled during the Tang Dynasty

Huang Di (Yellow Emperor) legendary Chinese emperor and father of traditional Chinese medicine

Huizong eighth ruler of the Song Dynasty; a poet, painter, calligrapher, and musician, he wrote the *Daguanchalun* (Treatise on Tea)

Jingdi ruler of the Han Dynasty; father of Prince Liu Sheng

Jing Hao important landscape painter and writer of the Five Dynasties era (also known as the Ten Kingdoms Period)

Kublai Khan fifth and last ruler of the Mongol Empire who founded the Yuan Dynasty

Prince Liu Sheng son of Emperor Jingdi, sixth emperor of the Han Dynasty; Jingdi gave Liu Sheng his own state of Zhongshan to rule over

Princess Tou Wan wife of Liu Sheng, Prince of Zhongshan

Ruan Ji third-century poet, one of a group of poets and philosophers who retreated to a life in the countryside to escape the rules and politics of life at court

Shi Huangdi founder and first ruler of the Qin Dynasty, which unified China for the first time

Shi Zhengzhi government official during the Song Dynasty

Wang Hui renowned landscape painter during the late Ming and early Qing dynasties

Wang Ximeng important landscape painter during the Song Dynasty

Wu Di seventh emperor of the Han Dynasty who greatly increased China's territory and organized a strong, centralized Confucian state

Wuzong fifteenth emperor of the Tang Dynasty

Xuanzong seventh and longest-reigning emperor of the Tang Dynasty, whose reign ended in the An Lushan rebellion

Xunzi Confucian philosopher during the Warring States Period who believed that people could improve their character through education and ritual

Yang Guifei favorite concubine of Emperor Xuanzong of the Tang Dynasty, killed during the An Lushan rebellion

Zhang Sheng military commander during the Sui Dynasty

Zhu Qiyu seventh emperor of the Ming Dynasty

Glossary

Abrade wear down or rub smooth through friction, such as with sand or sandpaper

Adjutant military officer who acts as an assistant to a higher-ranking officer

Bodhisattva compassionate, wise, and loving person on the final path to spiritual enlightenment who chooses to remain on earth to save others rather than achieve nirvana

Bureaucracy administration of government through fixed rules and procedures, and organized into various departments and offices staffed with officials at varying levels of authority

Calligraphy the art of fine, stylized, or artistic handwriting using a pen, or a brush and ink; considered as important as painting in Chinese culture

Celadon particular type of green crackle glaze that was first used in China and ranges in color from very pale to deep jade; the stoneware and pottery decorated with this glaze

Ceramic hard, brittle material made by shaping and firing minerals such as clay at high temperatures; the products made from this material, such as pottery, earthenware, and porcelain

Circumference the distance around the outside of an object, shape, or place

Cloisonné decorative enamelwork in which delicate metal wire is welded onto objects such as jewelry, bowls, and vases to form a design, then filled in with enamel paste in various colors; this is fired, then smoothed and polished

Concubine additional wife living with a man of higher social status, but who does not have the status and legal rights of an official wife

Cosmos the entire world (or universe) and everything in it

Dynasty succession or series of rulers who descend from the same family

Filigree detailed ornamental work made from fine wire, often gold or silver, which is twisted and bent into intricate shapes; most commonly used for jewelry

Frieze sculpted or carved horizontal band running along the outside of a building or wall, or around a room

Geometric of or relating to art or designs based on simple shapes, such as lines, squares, and circles

Hierarchy arrangement of people or things by increasing or decreasing levels or positions of relative importance, power, or status

Kaolin type of fine, usually white clay used to make ceramic ware

Lacquered coated with a smooth clear varnish with a glossy finish

Mandolin small musical instrument from the lute family with four to six strings, a pear-shaped body with a rounded bottom, and a straight neck similar to a guitar

Nephrite silicate mineral that is white to dark green—and sometimes blue or black—in color; one of two types of jade, a semi-precious stone

Nirvana concept found in Buddhism and Hinduism; ultimate state of perfect spiritual enlightenment, filled with joy, wisdom, and compassion, and free from the pain, desires, and passions of human existence

Pagoda towerlike building made of wood, brick, or stone which has several stories, each with a roof that curves up at the outer edges; often built as a Buddhist temple or shrine, or as part of a monastery complex

Porcelain hard, mostly white translucent ceramic made by firing clay (usually kaolin) and other materials in a kiln at high temperatures

Shaman a person who acts as a link or channel between the human world and the spirit world in some religions, and is able to communicate with the unseen world of gods, demons, and ancestor spirits

Stele (pl. stelae) stone or slab that stands upright whose surface is inscribed, engraved or sculpted with writing, symbols, or pictures, used as a monument or commemorative tablet

Steppe huge flat and mostly treeless area covered in grasslands, found in parts of Central Asia, Southeastern Europe, and Siberia

Stupa Buddhist monument or shrine

Terracotta literally means "baked earth"; coarse clay that is fired in a kiln to become hard pottery or ceramic ware that is usually brownish orange in color and left unglazed

Torso trunk of the body; the human body without head, neck, arms, and legs

Translucent allowing light to pass through

Wattle twigs, reeds, or branches woven to form walls, roofs, and fences

Yang male aspect of the universal energy or life force (*qi*) represented by light, heat, and dryness

Yin feminine aspect of the universal energy or life force (*qi*) represented by darkness, coolness, and wetness

Zither type of stringed musical instrument with a shallow soundbox

Learn More About

Books

Anderson, Dale. *Ancient China (History in Art).* Chicago: Raintree, 2005

Art, Suzanne Strauss. *The Story of Ancient China.* Lincoln, Mass: Pemblewick Press, 2001

Art, Suzanne Strauss. *China's Later Dynasties.* Lincoln, Mass: Pemblewick Press, 2002

Barnhart, R et al. *Three Thousand Years of Chinese Painting.* New Haven: Yale University Press, 2002

Ciarla, Roberto. *The Eternal Army: The Terracotta Army of the First Chinese Emperor (Timeless Treasures).* Vercelli: White Star, 2005

Cotterell, Arthur & Buller, Laura. *Ancient China (DK Eyewitness Books).* New York: Dorling Kindersley, 2005

Gascoigne, Bamber. *The Dynasties of China: A History.* Philadelphia, PA: Running Press 2003

Hearn, Maxwell. *How to Read Chinese Paintings (Metropolitan Museum of Art).* New York: Metropolitan Museum of Art, 2008

Hollihan-Elliot, Sheila. *Art and Architecture of China: The History and Culture of China.* Broomall, PA: Mason Crest Publishers, 2005

O'Connor, Jane. *The Emperor's Silent Army: Terracotta Warriors of Ancient China.* New York: Viking Juvenile, 2002

Shuter, Jane. *Ancient Chinese Art (Art in History).* Chicago: Heinemann Library, 2006

Web Sites

Asian Historical Architecture www.orientalarchitecture.com/

The Berger Foundation—Slide Library of Architectural Sites www.bergerfoundation.ch/wat1/Achine

British Museum, London—Online catalogue www.britishmuseum.org/explore/world_cultures.aspx

China page—Chinese Painting http://www.chinapage.com/paint1.html

History for Kids—Chinese Art www.historyforkids.org/learn/china/art/index.htm

The Huntington Archive—Online Catalogue http://kaladarshan.arts.ohio-state.edu/China/ChIndx.html

Museum of Fine Arts, Boston—Online Catalogue www.mfa.org/collections/index.asp?key=21

National Palace Museum, Taiwan—Online Catalogue www.npm.gov.tw/en/collection/selections_01.htm

Nelson-Atkins Museum of Art—Online Catalogue www.nelson-atkins.org/art/Chinese.cfm

The Palace Museum, Beijing—Online Catalogue www.dpm.org.cn/English/default.asp

Shanghai Museum—Online Catalogue www.shanghaimuseum.net/en/index.asp

Index